Congressional
Research
Service

Human Rights in China and U.S. Policy

Thomas Lum
Specialist in Asian Affairs

July 18, 2011

Congressional Research Service

7-5700

www.crs.gov

RL34729

CRS Report for Congress

Prepared for Members and Committees of Congress

Summary

This report examines human rights conditions in China, including the 2011 crackdown on rights activists and dissent; ongoing human rights abuses; recent PRC efforts to protect human rights; and the development of civil society. Ongoing human rights problems in China include the excessive use of violence by public security forces, unlawful detention, torture of detainees, arbitrary use of state security laws against political dissidents, coercive family planning policies, state control of information, and religious and ethnic persecution. Tibetans, Uighur Muslims, and Falun Gong adherents have been singled out for especially harsh treatment. For additional, comprehensive information about human rights conditions in China, see the Congressional-Executive Commission on China, *Annual Report 2010*, and the U.S. Department of State, *2010 Human Rights Report: China*.

The Chinese leadership's resistance to major political reform and fuller support of civil liberties has been driven largely by its fears of social unrest and political instability. Moreover, some public opinion surveys suggest that many Chinese people, while wanting greater freedoms, do not support rapid political change. Nonetheless, Chinese society has become more assertive. Incidents of social protests are frequent, numerous, and widespread. Economic, social, and demographic changes have given rise to labor unrest. PRC citizens have become increasingly aware of their legal rights, while emerging networks of lawyers, journalists, and activists have advanced the causes of many aggrieved individuals and groups. The mass media continues to push the boundaries of officially approved discourse, and the Internet has made it impossible for the government to restrict information as fully as before.

The PRC government has attempted to respond to some popular grievances, develop the legal system, and cautiously support the expansion of civil society, while suppressing activists who attempt to organize mass protests and dissidents who openly question sensitive policies or call for fundamental political change. This approach has produced modest improvements in some human rights conditions, but also allowed for continued, serious abuses. In recent months, the government has intensified efforts to suppress legal activists, rights defenders, and other individuals and groups whom it has deemed to be threatening to social and political stability.

The United States government has developed a comprehensive array of policy tools aimed toward promoting democracy, human rights, and the rule of law in China, but their effects have been felt primarily along the margins of the PRC political system. U.S. government efforts to promote human rights in China have included sanctions; openly criticizing PRC human rights policies and calling for the release of political prisoners; bilateral dialogue; "quiet diplomacy;" and hearings and investigations. The U.S. Congress has appropriated funding for democracy, human rights, rule of law, environmental, and other programs in China, including Tibet, and supported Internet freedom and public diplomacy efforts aimed at the PRC. Some policy makers contend that U.S. engagement with China has failed to produce meaningful political reform and improvements in human rights conditions. Other experts argue that engagement has helped to advance economic and social change in China, to develop social and legal foundations for democracy and human rights, and to open channels through which to directly communicate U.S. concerns.

Contents

Contacts

Overview

Human rights conditions in the People's Republic of China (PRC) remain a central issue in U.S.-China relations. For many U.S. policy-makers, progress in this area represents a test of the success of U.S. engagement with China, particularly since permanent normal trade relations (PNTR) status was established in 2000. Some analysts contend that the U.S. policy of engagement with China has failed to produce meaningful political reform, and that without fundamental progress in this area, the bilateral relationship will remain unstable. Others argue that U.S. engagement has helped to accelerate economic and social change and build social and legal foundations for democracy and the advancement of human rights in the PRC.

Many observers argue that violations of civil liberties and cases of political and religious persecution in China have increased in recent years, the leadership remains authoritarian, and economic development, based largely upon trade with the United States, has strengthened the Communist government rather than empowered the people.[1] Other analysts and many Chinese citizens contend that economic and social freedoms have grown considerably, the government's control over most aspects of people's lives has receded, opportunities for providing opinions on policy have increased, and rights activism has sprouted. Disagreements over whether progress has been made often stem from differences over which indicators are emphasized, such as central government policies, local government actions, civil society, or short-term versus long-term trends. In many ways, growing government restrictions on political, religious, and other freedoms and greater assertion of civil rights have occurred simultaneously.

Major Themes

This findings of this report reflect the following themes:

- A crackdown on dissent in 2011 has been attributed to the government's nervousness about continued outbreaks of social unrest, growing rights activism, the upcoming PRC leadership change in 2012-2013, and the potential for Arab Spring-inspired anti-government demonstrations. Some analysts also blame decreasing leverage by the United States on Chinese human rights policies. It is not yet clear how recent PRC government actions will affect social stability, civil society, public opinion, and political reform in China in the medium term. Some experts view the crackdown as representing one of the largest setbacks for liberalization in China since an attempt to launch a new political party, the China Democracy Party, was squelched and its leaders imprisoned in 1998. Other observers argue that due to the greater political assertiveness of the Chinese people compared to a decade ago, the government likely will seek to avoid a popular backlash, by limiting its repressive actions to selected key activists and dissidents.

- The PRC government has compromised little, if at all, on popular demands that it perceives to represent challenges to its authority. Serious human rights abuses continue in many areas. The PRC government has shown itself to be particularly intolerant of political dissent, freedom of speech, independent social and religious organizations,

---

[1] For a variation of this view, see James Mann, *The China Fantasy: How Our Leaders Explain Away Chinese Repression*, New York: Viking, 2006.

resistance to government policies from Tibetans, Uighurs, and Falun Gong adherents, and challenges to the official verdict of the 1989 Tiananmen democracy movement.

- Many Chinese citizens have experienced some marginal improvements in human rights protections and rights activism has increased. These changes have come about through both government policies and the development of civil society. The government has enacted laws to acknowledge or try to prevent some of the most egregious violations of human rights and abuses of power, strengthened the legal system, and often publicly sympathized with some aggrieved citizens. Social groups have engaged in protests to defend their rights, often aided by journalists, lawyers, and activists whose activities put them at risk of physical harm, loss of their professional licenses, harassment of themselves and their families, and imprisonment.

- The Internet has provided Chinese citizens with unprecedented amounts of information and the opportunity to express opinions publicly. Due to government censorship and other controls and to the non-political nature of most web activity in China, the Internet has proven to be less of a political factor than many observers had expected or hoped. Nonetheless, the Internet has made it impossible for the government to restrict information as fully as before. In many cases, news disseminated independently online has helped to hold government officials more accountable than in the past.

- The following social variables could potentially provide impetus for political reform in China: A shift in public concerns from local and economic issues to national, political ones; the growth of protest activity that includes not only socially and economically marginalized groups, such as farmers, workers, and migrant laborers, but also the urban middle class, professionals, and private entrepreneurs; linkages among social groups; and the development of new communications media and counter-censorship technologies.

- The U.S. government has developed a comprehensive array of tactics and programs aimed at promoting democracy, human rights, and the rule of law in China, but their effects have been felt primarily along the margins of the PRC political system. Some experts argue that these policies have had little impact, and are constrained by the overarching policy of U.S. diplomatic and economic engagement with China. Other observers contend that U.S. human rights and engagement policies have helped to set conditions in place in China that are necessary for progress and have helped the U.S. government to remain involved in the process.

"Responsive Authoritarianism"

The People's Republic of China is an authoritarian state in which the permanent leadership role of the Chinese Communist Party (CCP) is inscribed in the Constitution, and the legislative and judicial branches lack the power to check the CCP and the state. Recent speeches by PRC leaders have indicated that the CCP fully intends to maintain its monopoly in power. Although Premier Wen Jiabao, who is thought to be relatively liberal, has advocated deepening political reforms and expanding direct popular elections at the local levels, he has not called for radical change, but rather for incremental progress under the leadership of the CCP.[2] The PRC Constitution protects

---

[2] Keith Richburg, "China's Premier Again Calls for Political Reform," *Washington Post*, March 14, 2011.

many civil liberties, including the freedoms of speech, press, association, assembly, and religious belief, but these rights for the most part are not respected in practice. The government regards these ends as subordinate to the CCP's authority and to the policy goals of maintaining state security and social stability, promoting economic development, and providing for economic and social rights. The CCP leadership denounces foreign criticisms of its human rights policies as interference in China's internal affairs, and asserts that perspectives on human rights vary according a country's level of economic development and social system."[3]

Under the leadership of CCP General Secretary and President Hu Jintao and Premier Wen Jiabao, both in office since 2003, the PRC government has developed along the lines of what some scholars call "responsive authoritarianism."[4] It has striven to become more responsive, accountable, and law-based. Chinese leaders also have become more sensitive to popular views, particularly those expressed on the Internet. However, the government has rejected political reforms that might challenge its monopoly on power, and continued to respond forcefully to signs and instances of social instability, autonomous social organization, and independent political activity. Although the government has made some progress in enacting laws aimed at curbing some of the most egregious human rights abuses, it has not created or strengthened institutions that would help enforce these laws, such as checks and balances and genuine popular elections beyond the village level. Furthermore, many lawyers, activists, and journalists seeking to protect people's rights or expose violations of them have been harassed or imprisoned by authorities. PRC leaders have tolerated some mass demonstrations against government officials and policies, particularly at the local level, but also have arrested protest leaders. Communist Party and state officials have retained a significant degree of arbitrary authority, and corruption has negated many efforts to improve governance.

U.S. Government Policy

Many experts and policy makers have sharply disagreed over the best policy approaches and methods to apply toward human rights issues in China. Differing U.S. goals include promoting fundamental political change in the PRC and supporting incremental progress. Possible approaches range from placing human rights conditions upon the bilateral relationship to inducing democratic change through bilateral and international engagement. Policy tools include private discussions; sanctions; open criticism of PRC human rights policies; coordinating international pressure; support of and contact with dissidents; bilateral dialogue; human rights, democracy, and related programs; promoting Internet freedom; public diplomacy efforts; and monitoring and highlighting human rights abuses.

Since the end of the 1980s, successive U.S. administrations have employed broadly similar strategies for promoting human rights in China. Some analysts have referred to the U.S. foreign policy approach of promoting democracy in China through diplomatic and economic engagement, without directly challenging Communist Party rule, as a strategy of "peaceful evolution."[5]

---

[3] Information Office of the State Council, the People's Republic of China, "Progress in China's Human Rights in 2009," *Xinhua*, September 26, 2010; "Beijing Working on Human Rights Plan," *South China Morning Post*, July 13, 2011.

[4] For example, see Robert P. Weller, "Responsive Authoritarianism," in Bruce Gilley and Larry Diamond, eds., *Political Change in China: Comparisons with Taiwan*, Boulder: Lynne Reinner Publishers, 2008.

[5] Warren Christopher, Secretary of State under the Clinton Administration (1993-1997), stated: "Our policy will seek to facilitate a peaceful evolution of China from communism to democracy by encouraging the forces of economic and (continued...)

President Bill Clinton referred to this policy as "constructive engagement" – furthering diplomatic and economic ties while pressing for open markets and democracy, calling it "our best hope to secure our own interest and values and to advance China's."[6] President George W. Bush also came to view U.S. engagement as the most effective means of promoting U.S. interests and freedom in China.[7]

The Obama Administration

As China's importance in global economic, security, environmental, and other matters has grown, both the Bush and Obama Administrations aimed to forge bilateral cooperation on many fronts, while disagreeing deeply with Beijing on many human rights issues. In remarks during the summit with PRC President Hu Jintao in January 2011, President Obama referred to the universality of the freedoms of speech, assembly, and religion, a point frequently made by President Clinton. Echoing a theme evoked by President Bush in his second term, President Obama also suggested that greater respect for human rights in China would benefit China's success and global stability.[8]

In December 2009, Secretary of State Hillary Clinton described the Administration's human rights policy as one of "principled pragmatism." This policy is based upon the premise that tough but quiet diplomacy is both less disruptive to the overall relationship and more effective in producing change than public censure.[9] Some policy observers have admonished President Obama for reducing the prominence of human rights in U.S. policy toward China and favoring other concerns, such as economic, security, and environmental issues. Other analysts have argued that Sino-U.S. cooperation in these areas creates greater and more favorable opportunities for promoting human rights in the PRC. Some critics have pointed to a number of actions (or inactions) by the Administration, including the postponement of a White House meeting with the Dalai Lama until after President Obama's trip to China in November 2009, and Secretary Clinton's February 2009 statement that pressing Beijing on human rights issues "can't interfere" with other key areas of the relationship. Some policy makers also have criticized the Administration for producing too few concessions, such as political prisoner releases, by the PRC government.[10]

Nonetheless, the Administration has pressed China on human rights issues, both privately and openly. During his visit to China in November 2009, President Obama briefly spoke about human

---

(...continued)

political liberalization in that great country." Warren Christopher, Statement before the Senate Foreign Relations Committee, January 13, 1993.

[6] Clinton Defends 'Constructive Engagement' Of China CNN.com October 24, 1997.

[7] "Transcript of Bob Costas' Interview with President George W. Bush," *PRNewsChannel.com*, August 11, 2008; "Bush Woos China on Trade," *BBC News*, May 30, 2001.

[8] Ewen MacAskill and Tania Branigan, "Obama Presses Hu Jintao on Human Rights During White House Welcome," *Guardian.co.uk*, January 19, 2011; Helene Cooper and Mark Landler, "Obama Pushes Hu on Rights but Stresses Ties to China," *New York Times*, January 19, 2011.

[9] Elise Labott, "Clinton Defends Stance on Human Rights," *CNN*.com, March 11, 2009; Charley Keyes, "U.S. is 'Pragmatic' with China, Russia," *CNN.com*, December 15, 2009.

[10] On February 25, 2009, Secretary of State Hillary Clinton asserted: "We have to continue to press them but our pressing on those issues can't interfere with the global economic crisis, the global climate change crisis and the security crises. We have to have a dialog that leads to an understanding and cooperation on each of those."

rights and Internet freedom during a town hall meeting with university students in Shanghai. Although the broadcast of the speech was limited to Shanghai and transcripts on the Internet were censored, thousands of Chinese reportedly accessed the White House website and cheered Obama's appeal for Internet freedom.[11] Secretary Clinton has spoken out on human rights issues, including criticizing China's Internet censorship and alleged hacking of U.S. companies in January 2010, demanding Nobel laureate Liu Xiaobo's release from prison in October 2010, calling for the release of dissident artist Ai Weiwei in April 2011, and discussing China's human rights record, calling it "deplorable," in a June 2011 interview.[12] In July 2011, President Obama met with the Dalai Lama at the White House and reiterated his support for human rights in Tibet and for dialogue between the Dalai Lama and Beijing.

Congressional Actions

The U.S. Congress has been at the forefront of maintaining human rights as a pillar of U.S. policy toward the PRC, through such measures and efforts as sanctions, resolutions, hearings, and democracy assistance in support of human rights in China and in Tibet. Congress legislated sanctions following the Tiananmen military crackdown in 1989 and has withheld support for United Nations Population Fund programs in China. Members of Congress have introduced resolutions calling attention to human rights abuses in the PRC, including the imprisonment and detention of political, religious, and minority figures; persecution of Tibetans, Uighurs, and Falun Gong adherents; censorship of the Internet and other mass media; coercive abortions; and China's deportation of North Korean refugees. Congressional committees, the Tom Lantos Human Rights Commission, the Congressional-Executive Commission on China, the U.S. Commission on International Religious Freedom, and other congressionally mandated bodies and fora have investigated, publicized, and reported on human rights conditions in China. Foreign operations appropriations measures have authorized and funded democracy, human rights, and rule of law programs in the PRC; economic, cultural, and environmental programs in Tibet; and Internet freedom efforts in China and other countries.

Recent Developments

Crackdown on Dissent

In the winter and spring of 2011, the PRC government intensified efforts to suppress China's increasingly active civil society, including rights defenders, activist lawyers, bloggers and other critical voices, non-governmental organizations (NGOs), independent churches, restive ethnic minority groups, and others whom it deemed threatening to social and political stability. Chinese security forces reportedly detained, arrested, or held incommunicado between 50 and 100 people, including 20 who face prosecution for subversion, and placed another roughly 200 people under heavy surveillance for political reasons.[13] According to many experts, the breadth and intensity of

---

[11] Charles Hutzler and Jennifer Loven, "Analysis: Obama's China Trip Shows Power Shifting," *Associated Press*, November 17, 2009; Charles Hutzler and Jennifer Loven, "Obama's Visit to China Yields Few Concessions," *Associated Press*, November 18, 2009; Francois Bougon, "Obama's Visit Leaves Dissidents Disappointed," *Agence France-Presse*, November 19, 2009.

[12] Jeffrey Goldberg, "Danger: Falling Tyrants," *The Atlantic*, June 2011.

[13] Nicholas Bequelin, "Crackdown in China," *International Herald Tribune*, April 7, 2011; Mary Hennock, "In China, (continued...)

the crackdown in 2011 is unprecedented under the current PRC leadership. Recent major events and cases include large police presences in Beijing and Shanghai in February 2011 in attempts to head off Middle East-inspired anti-government demonstrations, and the April 2011 arrest of one of China's best-known artists and government critics, Ai Weiwei, for tax evasion and other charges. (Ai was released on June 22, 2011.) The Congressional-Executive Commission on China provides a list of people targeted in the crackdown.[14]

The recent spate of arrests appeared to be part of a broader and longer-term policy of adapting to and regulating a fast-changing and increasingly dynamic society while selectively applying tactics of intimidation and coercion against individuals and groups that the state perceives to be challenging or publicly questioning its authority or control. Several indicators support this trend. The number of people arrested for endangering state security, the most serious political crime, was over 950 in 2010, according to one estimate, of which a majority were Tibetans and Uighurs charged with "splittism" and related crimes.[15] This number represents a 44% decline from 2008, when protests in Tibetan regions and preparations for the Beijing Olympics gave rise to many arrests, but still a substantial increase from pre-2008 levels.[16] PRC public security officials reportedly issued statements in 2009-2010 in support of an "indefinite extension of a security crackdown" aimed at "safeguarding social stability," while the government has bolstered the budget and capacity of the police forces.[17] State control methods reportedly have increasingly made use of coercive, extra-judicial tactics, including physical harassment or beatings by plain-clothes agents, forced disappearances, and threats against and harassment of family members.

The PRC government's recent attempts to silence its critics and subdue social forces have been widely attributed to the recent political unrest in the Middle East and the CCP's fear of similar, large-scale protests at home. Some experts argue that the PRC government has done a better job of satisfying public demands for economic opportunity and social justice than many Middle Eastern governments, and that political movements on a national scale are unlikely. Nonetheless, China's leaders, who face a leadership transition in 2012-2013, have reason to be concerned about their ability to respond to democratic forces in the society. Deep and manifold popular grievances against mostly local government officials are well-documented—roughly 90,000-100,000 "mass protests" have been reported annually in the past several years. In 2010, there were 72 "major" incidents of social unrest, according to a Chinese study, a 20% increase from the previous year.[18] Awareness of legal and human rights among Chinese citizens, in some ways

---

(...continued)

Political Chill Begins to Reach Universities," *Chronicle of Higher Education*, May 3, 2011.

[14] "Authorities Crack Down on Rights Defenders, Lawyers, Artists, and Bloggers," *Congressional-Executive Commission on* China, May 3, 2011, http://www.cecc.gov/index.php; Peter Ford, "Report on China's 'Jasmine Revolution'? Not If You Want Your Visa," *Yahoo! News*, March 3, 2011; "Jasmine Activists Charged," *Radio Free Asia*, February 25, 2011; Anita Chang, "China Tries to Stamp Out 'Jasmine Revolution'," *Associated Press*, February 20, 2011.

[15] "Chinese Government Appears to Halt Sentence Reductions for Political Prisoners," *Dui Hua Human Rights Journal*, February 22, 2011.

[16] "Official Data Show State Security Arrests, Prosecution Remained at Historic Levels in 2010," *Dui Hua News*, March 15, 2011.

[17] "Top Chinese Security Officials Urge Continued Crackdown in 2010," *Congressional-Executive Commission on China*, February 12, 2010; Dean Cheng, "China's Crackdown and America's Response: Supporting Liberty in Distant Places," *Heritage Foundation WebMemo No. 3221* (April 11, 2011).

[18] Francis Fukuyama, "Is China Next?" *Wall Street Journal*, March 12, 2011, citing a report from Jiao Tong University (China).

promoted by the government, continues to grow, while a small but increasing number of activists, lawyers, journalists, and others has continued to champion human rights causes.[19]

Jasmine Revolution

In February 2011, an online appeal that appeared to be authored by Chinese activists overseas called on people in China to take part in a "Jasmine Revolution"—peaceful "protest walks" in major cities on consecutive Sundays—to highlight the desire for greater democracy in China in light of popular movements sweeping the Middle East. Although a few hundred protesters reportedly were turned away by public security forces from the main city square in Shanghai, uniformed and plainclothes police and curious onlookers appeared to far outnumber demonstrators in Beijing, while in other cities there was little if any protest activity. Government authorities reportedly detained dozens of human rights activists and lawyers, charged several prominent dissidents with subversion, and physically assaulted and threatened foreign reporters.

Nobel Laureate Liu Xiaobo

In October 2010, the Nobel Committee awarded Liu Xiaobo, formerly a professor at Beijing Normal University and a long time political dissident, activist, and writer, the Nobel Peace Prize for his "long and non-violent struggle for fundamental human rights." He had spent three years in prison for his role in the 1989 democracy movement and three years in a labor camp (1996-1999) for openly questioning Communist Party rule. From 2003 to 2007, Liu served as President of the Independent Chinese PEN Center, which advocates freedom of speech and press, and experienced frequent harassment by local authorities. In December 2008, Liu helped draft "Charter '08" commemorating the 60th anniversary of the United Nations' adoption of the Universal Declaration of Human Rights.[20] The document, signed by 300 Chinese citizens and posted on the Internet, called for human rights and fundamental changes in China's political system. It eventually garnered roughly 10,000 additional signatures online. The PRC government shut down the Charter's website, harassed, interrogated, or denied career benefits to dozens of signatories, and arrested Liu. In December 2009, a Beijing court sentenced Liu to 11 years in prison on charges of "inciting subversion of state power."

Following the announcement of the Nobel Peace Prize, the PRC government harassed, detained, interrogated, placed under house arrest, denied visas to, and confiscated the computer equipment of dozens of fellow Chinese dissidents, political activists, and family members. It barred members and representatives of Liu's family from traveling to Oslo to accept the prize, and blocked western news media in the days leading up to the awards ceremony.[21] The PRC government also reportedly lobbied foreign governments, warning them not to send diplomats to the Nobel ceremony.

---

[19] Linda Yeung, "Reform School," *South China Morning Post*, November 28, 2010.

[20] "Charter '08" was inspired by "Charter 77," the Czechoslovakian democratic movement.

[21] "Keith B. Richburg, "On Eve of Nobel Ceremony, China Cracks Down and Lashes Out," *Washington Post*, December 9, 2010.

Labor Issues

In the spring and summer of 2010, China experienced a surge in labor disputes and unrest, including three dozen strikes at Foxconn, Honda, Hyundai, and other foreign-owned factories in Guangdong province. In addition, many less-noticed labor incidents occurred "everywhere" and in "all kinds of enterprises."[22] These developments indicated an evolving relationship between workers, enterprises, and the government. Wage pressures—caused by China's economic development, a shortage of young workers due to demographic changes, the rising value of the *renminbi*, and greater enforcement of the 2008 Labor Contract Law—coupled with widening income disparities, a growing awareness of rights, and rising expectations among China's new generation of workers, helped to fuel the unrest.[23] At Taiwan electronics giant Foxconn, known as the world's largest supplier of components for global brands such as Apple, Microsoft, and Hewlett-Packard, strikes in some of its factories in China were preceded by the suicides of 11 Chinese employees earlier in the year.[24] Many observers and labor activists attributed the suicides to highly demanding and stressful working conditions.

Most labor protesters sought higher wages, improved working conditions, and enforcement of PRC labor laws, although some workers also demanded the right to elect their own union representatives or form their own unions. Some Chinese labor experts and official sources expressed support for higher wages, a greater advocacy role for China's official union, the All China Federation of Trade Unions (ACFTU), and the process of collective bargaining. Some legislative proposals at the provincial and national levels supported the right to strike.[25]

Compared to past labor movements in China, the strikes of 2010 were unusual for several reasons: the official media covered them; they resulted in positive results for many workers, such as substantial pay raises; labor organizers skillfully used Internet social networking tools; and, in some cases, management negotiated directly with strike leaders.[26] However, as in the past, the activism of workers did not represent a national labor or political movement. For the most part, workers did not organize on a long-term basis or build linkages between enterprises, and their aims were narrow or focused on wages and working conditions. Moreover, strikers at some enterprises exploited nationalistic or anti-Japanese sentiment, thereby reducing antagonism between labor and the government. China's leaders, meanwhile, remain vigilant against the development of a national labor movement, do not allow the formation of independent unions or democratic elections for ACFTU representatives, and have not adopted proposals to formally allow strikes. Roughly two dozen labor activists are known to be in jail.[27]

---

[22] Keith B. Richburg, "Labor Unrest Continues to Rise throughout China," *Washington Post*, June 12, 2010.

[23] Elaine Kurtenbach, "Companies Brace for End of Cheap Made-in-China Era," Associated Press, July 8, 2010; Keith Richburg, "Labor Unrest in China Reflects Changing Demographics, More Awareness of Rights," *Washington Post*, June 7, 2010.

[24] Foxconn reportedly has more than 20 factories in China and 920,000 employees. Frederik Balfour and Tim Culpan, "Inside Foxconn," *Businessweek*, September 19, 2010.

[25] According to PRC law and policy, there is no constitutional right to strike. Peng Pu, "Drive to Give Trade Unions Stronger Role," *Global Times*, August 30, 2010; Dexter Roberts, "Is the Right to Strike Coming to China?" *Bloomberg Businessweek*, August 5, 2010.

[26] Li Qiaoyi, "Labor Issues Top the Agenda," *Global Times*, June 28, 2010.

[27] U.S. Department of State, *2010 Human Rights Report: China*, April 8, 2011.

A Mixed Picture

The past few years have witnessed a mixed picture regarding human rights conditions in China. On the one hand, human rights organizations and commissions have reported worsening and deteriorating conditions in China. None of the groups known to suffer the greatest persecution by the PRC government has experienced real improvement in overall treatment, according to reports. These groups include Tibetans and ethnic Uighur (Uygur) Muslims, leaders of unsanctioned Christian churches, Falun Gong practitioners, political dissidents, and human rights defenders. The Nobel Committee's award of the 2010 Peace Prize to jailed dissident Liu Xiaobo, which the PRC government denounced as a western political ploy to weaken China, highlighted the Chinese leadership's deep resistance to change. On the other hand, the PRC government has continued to enact laws and policies aimed at reducing some of the most egregious human rights abuses, protecting property and labor rights, and promoting government transparency and citizen input. Moreover, the official press has become more critical of some human rights abuses.

Major Human Rights Issues

Major, ongoing human rights violations in China include the following: excessive use of violence by security forces and their proxies; unlawful and abusive detention; torture; arbitrary use of state security laws against political dissidents; coercive family planning policies; state control of information; harassment and persecution of people involved in unsanctioned religious activities, including worship in unregistered Protestant "house churches" and Catholic churches that express loyalty to the Pope; and mistreatment and deportation of North Korean refugees. Many Tibetans, Uighurs, and Falun Gong adherents have been singled out for especially harsh treatment.

The following ongoing human rights abuses, some of which are discussed at greater length elsewhere in this report, represent a selection of human rights issues in China.[28]

- Harassment, beatings by public security forces and government agents, house arrest, and unlawful detentions of petitioners, protest leaders, human rights attorneys, journalists, dissidents, and others.

- Unlawful killings of persons in state custody; family members generally are not allowed to investigate the causes of such deaths.[29]

- Physical abuse and the use of torture by the state against political detainees and criminal suspects, often resulting in forced confessions or renunciations of faith, despite government efforts to reduce such practices.

- Arbitrary use of state security laws against political dissidents, Tibetans, Uighur Muslims, Internet bloggers, and others.

- Sporadic reports of coercive abortions, forced sterilizations, and other related, unlawful government actions against women.

---

[28] For more complete descriptions of human rights abuses, see Congressional-Executive Commission on China, *Annual Report 2010*, October 10, 2010, and U.S. Department of State, *2010 Human Rights Report: China*, April 8, 2011.

[29] Ibid. For example, in April 2009, the *Supreme* People's Procuratorate (SPP) disclosed that at least 15 prisoners died unnatural deaths under unusual circumstances during the year and announced a plan to educate police on proper jail procedures. Austin Ramzy, "In China, Suspicious Jail Deaths on the Rise," *Time.com*, April 30, 2009.

- Strict controls over and punishments for public speech, discussion, and reporting of politically sensitive topics, such as the Tiananmen events of 1989, Taiwan relations, Tibet, Falun Gong, and the legitimacy of the Chinese Communist Party.

- Harassment and arrests of Christians worshipping in unofficial churches.

- Detention and arrests of Tibetans and Uighur Muslims suspected of engaging in "splittist" and other anti-government activities.

- Persecution of Falun Gong adherents.

- Repatriation of North Korean nationals residing in China, who likely face severe forms of punishment after returning North Korea, in violation of the U.N. Refugee Convention and its protocols.

Prisoners of Conscience

The *Dui Hua Foundation*, a non-profit organization that reports on human rights issues and monitors prisoners of conscience—political and religious prisoners and detainees—in China, estimates that there are roughly 25,000 such individuals in prisons, reeducation through labor (RTL) centers, and other facilities. The vast majority were sentenced for involvement with "cults" such as Falun Gong, endangering state security, or committing "counterrevolutionary" crimes. Sentences for state security crimes are relatively lengthy (5-15 years or longer), while many Falun Gong detainees have served one or more terms of up to 3-4 years in RTL camps.[30]

Forms of Illegal Detention

Many petitioners, generally citizens from rural areas who file complaints at petition offices in Beijing and provincial capitals seeking redress for government abuses and misconduct, reportedly are sent to secret detention centers or "black jails," where they lack legal protections and face a variety of abuses.[31] In Beijing alone, thousands of people reportedly are detained illegally in such facilities, which number between 50 and 73, each year.[32] Many petitioners, activists, dissidents, underground religious worshippers, Falun Gong practitioners, and others reportedly also have been held in psychiatric (*ankang*) hospitals for the criminally insane, where they have been forced to take medications, denied contact with their families, and subjected to rights abuses. In 2010, more than 100 Chinese lawyers reportedly urged the government to end the practice of detaining sane people in mental health facilities.[33]

Reeducation Through Labor

Reeducation through labor (*laojiao*) or RTL, an administrative measure, empowers the police to sentence persons found guilty of minor or non-criminal offenses, such as petty theft, prostitution, unlawful religious activity, and "disrupting social order," to a maximum of three to four years in

---

[30] Dui Hua Foundation, http://www.duihua.org.

[31] These abuses range from illegal land grabs and official corruption to police torture.

[32] An Alleyway in Hell: China's Abusive 'Black Jails,' *Human Rights Watch*, November 2009; Congressional-Executive Commission on China, *Annual Report 2010*, op. cit.

[33] Ibid.; Peter Ford, "China's Mental Hospitals: A New Push To Quash Dissent?" *Christian Science Monitor*, June 9, 2011.

labor camps without trial. Approximately 300 RTL centers holding roughly 250,000 people have absorbed large numbers of individuals deemed by the state to be a threat to social or political stability. According to some estimates, normally between 2% and 10% of the RTL population are being held for political reasons.[34] Many Falun Gong adherents were sent to RTL camps during the height of the crackdown a decade ago, at one time reportedly constituting up to half of all inmates.[35]

The National People's Congress and Party officials have openly discussed reforming the RTL system, including reducing the use of the measure, shortening terms, improving conditions, providing better legal protections for detainees, particularly minors, and providing better judicial oversight. In 2010, two Chinese legal scholars debated reforming the RTL system in a series of editorials. [36]

Americans Detained in China

Xue Feng, a China-born, naturalized U.S. citizen, was arrested in Beijing in 2007 on charges related to his acquisition of a Chinese database on China's oil industry while working for an American firm. In July 2010, after having been held incommunicado for a period and allegedly tortured, Xue was sentenced to eight years in prison for providing state secrets to foreigners. Xue claimed that he had believed the database to be commercially available. U.S. consular officials have had regular contact with Xue, although U.S. officials were denied access to Xue's November 2010 appeal hearing, in violation of the 1980 U.S.-China Consular Convention.[37] Another naturalized U.S. citizen, David Wei Dong, was sentenced in 2005 to 13 years in prison on the charge of espionage (spying for Taiwan). He is said to be in poor health. Dong's sentence was reduced by 18 months in 2010.

Human Rights Reforms/Legislation

While the government led by President Hu Jintao and Premier Wen Jiabao has placed more emphasis upon social stability and economic development than political reform, it has enacted major laws aimed at reducing some of the most serious patterns of human rights abuse. In 2004, the phrase, "the State respects and protects human rights" was added to the PRC Constitution. Laws and regulations designed to protect or promote human rights include those related to criminal defendants, the use of torture, the death penalty, labor conditions, private property, and government transparency and responsiveness. The PRC government's 9th White Paper on Human Rights reported that in 2009, procuratorial organs found 22,268 unlawful actions related to people

---

[34] Minnie Chan, "Kinder Face for Notorious Re-education Camps," *South China Morning Post*, February 21, 2007; Jim Yardley, "Issue in China: Many Jails Without Trial," *New York Times*, May 9, 2005.

[35] U.S. Department of State, *2009 Human Rights Report: China*, March 11, 2010; Falun Gong organizations have placed the number as far higher.

[36] Wu Jiao, "New Law to Abolish Laojiao System," *China Daily*, March 1, 2007; Jerome Cohen, "Legal Reform Can Promote Harmony," *South China Morning Post*, December 25, 2008; Congressional-Executive Commission on China, *Annual Report 2010*, op. cit.

[37] Embassy of the United States, Beijing, "DCM's Statement: Appeal Trial of Dr. Feng Xue," Press Release, October 30, 2010, http://beijing.usembassy-china.org.cn/113010dcm html.

in detention and prison and urged corrective actions to be taken on 337 cases of excessive detention.[38]

- **Rights of the Accused:** In July 2006, the state enacted prohibitions on specific acts of torture and requirements that interrogations of criminal suspects be video-recorded. These regulations followed a 2004 law forbidding the use of torture to obtain confessions. In 2010, the PRC government issued new rules and regulations intended to reduce physical abuses of detainees and inmates, including rejecting evidence obtained through torture, raising the accountability of state personnel for deaths and injuries sustained by people in their custody, and punishing police misconduct.[39] However, many reports of torture continue, and state compensation for wrongful detention and physical and mental abuse suffered by detainees remains the exception rather than the rule.

- **Organ Transplants:** In 2006 and 2007, PRC regulations banning trade in human organs went into effect. They stipulated that the donation of organs for transplant be free and voluntary. These restrictions followed growing evidence and international criticism of a booming and unregulated international trade in organs of executed Chinese prisoners, including what one report claimed were "large numbers" of Falun Gong practitioners.[40]

- **State Secrets Law:** In 2010, the PRC government amended legislation to reduce arbitrary use of the "state secrets" law and to make it easier for citizens to obtain compensation due to state negligence or abuse of power. However, according to most observers, the law remains vague and still can be used broadly against political dissidents and others.[41]

- **The Death Penalty:** According to Amnesty International and other groups, China is believed to execute several thousands of people each year. In March 2007, the Supreme People's Court was granted sole power to review and ratify all death sentences, following four years of discussion among the CCP leadership. In 2010, the National People's Congress amended the Criminal Law to reduce the number of crimes punishable by death from 68 to 55. In May 2011, the Supreme People's Court instructed lower courts to suspend death sentences for two years for "all cases that don't require immediate execution."[42]

- **Labor Rights:** In March 2007, China's legislature passed the Labor Contract Law to help enforce the rights of workers. The law, which went into effect in January 2008, reportedly spurred an initial dramatic rise in labor dispute arbitration cases and strikes.[43] After a period in which enforcement was

---

[38] Information Office of the State Council, op. cit.

[39] Congressional-Executive Commission on China, *Annual Report 2010*, op. cit.; U.S. Department of State, *2010 Human Rights Report*, op. cit.

[40] David Matas and David Kilgour, "Bloody Harvest: Revised Report into Allegations of Organ Harvesting of Falun Gong Practitioners in China," January 2007.

[41] In 2010, the PRC government announced that it had amended legislation on the protection of state secrets to clarify the definition of a state secret, reduce the level of protected information, and open some information to the public. Zhao Ran, "China Amends Law on State Secrets," *Global Times*, September 27, 2010.

[42] Michael Bristow, "China Orders Suspension of Death Sentences," *BBC News*, May 25, 2011.

[43] "China Rocked by Labor Disputes Due to Legal Reforms, Inflation Fears," *Nikkei Weekly*, July 14, 2008.

weakened due to the global economic crisis, the law was a catalyst for a new surge in labor unrest in 2010.

- **Property Rights:** In March 2007, the National People's Congress passed a constitutional amendment designed to protect property rights that had been debated since 2002. The new property law helps to protect private entrepreneurs, urban home owners, and farmers whose crop lands often risk seizure by government-backed real-estate developers.[44] In October 2008, the government issued new measures allowing farmers to lease and sell rights to use the property allocated to them by the state.[45]

- **Government Transparency:** In April 2007, the PRC government announced new rules requiring greater disclosure of official information.[46] In addition, institutional and legal mechanisms were established to provide for greater government responsiveness and accountability. In part, these measures represented attempts to compel local governments to reveal financial accounts related to land takings in rural areas.[47]

- **Government Responsiveness:** During the past several years, the government has sought greater public input on policy questions through consultation with experts and think tanks, public hearings, the Internet, and other channels. The Chinese Communist Party also has begun experimenting with soliciting recommendations on candidates for local Party positions.[48]

- **Human Rights Action Plan:** In April 2009, the PRC State Council released a two-year "action plan" that pledged an increased government commitment to human rights, including farmers' rights over land use, due process, freedom from torture, and expanded citizen participation and consultation. The government declared that its policy was designed to help bring China up to international standards as prescribed in the PRC Constitution, the Universal Declaration of Human Rights, and the International Covenant on Civil and Political Rights.[49] As the plan expired on December 31, 2010, many human rights activists criticized its limited scope, its emphasis on economic and social rather than political and civil rights, and continued human rights violations in China.[50] In July 2011, the State Council Information Office announced that the government was drawing up a four-year human rights plan which, as some analysts suggested, appeared designed primarily to address economic and social grievances.[51]

---

[44] Edward Cody, "Lawmakers Approve Measure to Protect Private Property," *Washington Post*, March 16, 2007.

[45] While the state owns all land in China, farmers are granted rights of use via long term (30-year) contracts with the state. Maureen Fan, "China to Allow Land Leasing, Transfer," *Washington Post*, October 20, 2008.

[46] Edward Cody, "China Announces Rules to Require Government Disclosures," *Washington Post*, April 24, 2007.

[47] Suisheng Zhao, "Political Reform in China: Toward Democracy or a Rule of Law Regime," *Asia Program Special Report No. 131*, Woodrow Wilson International Center for Scholars, June 2006; Richard Baum, "The Limits of Consultative Leninism," *Asia Program Special Report No. 131*, Woodrow Wilson International Center for Scholars, June 2006.

[48] Congressional-Executive Commission on China, *Annual Report 2010*, op. cit.

[49] The PRC has signed, but not ratified, the International Covenant on Civil and Political Rights.

[50] "China: Human Rights Action Plan Fails to Deliver," *Human Rights Watch*, January 11, 2011.

[51] "Beijing Working on Human Rights Plan," op. cit.

Civil Society

Although the Party remains the final, undisputed authority, non-state actors play a small but growing role in policy-making, political discourse, and social activity.[52] In some cases, the state has promoted civil society as a way to help promote social welfare. In other cases, civil society activists have pushed the boundaries of permissible social activity at great personal risk. Lawyers, journalists, and activists have been at the forefront in helping to protect and promote human rights and the public interest, although they have faced severe restrictions. They may form the beginnings of a small, loosely organized, and still largely latent human rights movement, in which "civil elites" work with grass roots groups to safeguard and promote rights.[53]

Social Organizations

The PRC government has expressed both an appreciation for the public contributions of social or civil society organizations (CSOs) and a wariness about their potential autonomy, intentions, and foreign contacts. Social organizations, which generally are required to be sponsored by a government agency, face complicated challenges related to their legality, financing, and political survival. According to PRC official estimates, China has over 430,000 registered social organizations, compared to 288,000 in 2004. When CSOs that are not officially registered are included, the total number of social organizations is estimated to be several million.[54] These groups include those that are state-administered, those that are formed outside of the government but have an official sponsor, those that register as businesses because they cannot secure a state sponsor, and unregistered student, community, and grassroots organizations.[55] Environmental groups have been at the forefront of the development of social organizations in China. Other areas in which CSOs operate include legal aid, public health, education, poverty alleviation, and rural development.

A Difficult Environment for Activist NGOs

In 2009, the Beijing government closed Open Constitution Initiative, a legal research center focusing on civil rights, while its founder and financial manager were detained.[56] In 2010, following over a decade of harassment, Wan Yanhai, a leading HIV/AIDS activist and founder of an AIDS awareness group, left China for the United States, expressing concerns for his personal safety. During the same year, Peking University reportedly terminated its sponsorship of the Center for Women's law and Legal Services because of the political implications and foreign funding of its activities.[57]

---

[52] Many "non-state" actors in China, such as scholars, non-governmental organizations, and private entrepreneurs, rely heavily upon the government for their livelihood or economic and political survival.

[53] Paul Mooney, "Beijing Silences 'One-Man Rights Organization'," *South China Morning Post*, January 27, 2008; Edward Cody, "In Chinese Uprisings, Peasants Find New Allies," *Washington Post*, November 26, 2005.

[54] Congressional-Executive Commission on China, *Annual Report 2010*, op. cit.

[55] Social organizations are required to register with an official or quasi-official sponsor, such as a state agency or educational institution. Unregistered social organizations are more vulnerable to arbitrary government policies, including closure, and are not eligible for tax exemptions. Some western analysts use the term "civil society organization" (CSO) rather than "non-governmental organization" to reflect the lack of autonomy from the state. The PRC government prefers the term "social organization" rather than CSO in order to avoid suggesting an adversarial relationship with the state.

[56] In May 2009, Open Constitution Initiative released a report rejecting the government's assertion that the Tibetan unrest of March 2008 was primarily instigated by the Dalai Lama, and pointing to causes related to social, cultural, and economic policies in the region. Congressional Executive Commission on China, *China Human Rights and Rule of Law Update*, Newsletter No. 4, 2009.

[57] Congressional-Executive Commission on China, *Annual Report 2010*, op. cit.

In the middle of the last decade, after nearly a decade of steady growth, Beijing began to tighten restrictions on social organizations while expressing suspicions about foreign funding and foreign NGOs operating in China. The government has been especially fearful of the potential for foreign NGOs to help foment political unrest, and reportedly established an office to monitor foreign NGOs and their Chinese partners. PRC leaders expressed the fear that China's fledgling civil society, combined with foreign "democracy assistance" and the involvement of international NGOs, could bring about a "color revolution."[58] In 2010, the PRC government continued to apply pressure on civil society groups through the "selective enforcement of regulations."[59]

The PRC government limits the potential growth and influence of civil society organizations through legal and extra-legal means. For example, PRC laws prohibit social organizations from establishing branches and engaging in public fundraising.[60] Many CSOs have come to rely heavily upon foreign grants. However, in 2010, the State Administration for Foreign Exchange issued a new set of requirements for accepting foreign donations, making it difficult for non-officially registered social organizations to accept foreign funding. The new rules also warned that such donations "shall not go against social morality or damage public interests and the legitimate rights and interests of other citizens."[61] The government has forbidden grants from some foreign democracy groups, and has punished politically provocative social organizations.

The industrial city of Shenzhen, bordering Hong Kong, has roughly 3,500 social organizations, more than double the national average per capita. In 2009, the municipality began to carry out reforms, in partnership with the Ministry of Civil Affairs, which have been debated but not enacted at the national level. The city has begun to ease legal restrictions on CSOs, allowing them to register without direct supervision by a government entity, to solicit funding within China and overseas, and to hire foreigners. Some labor groups in Shenzhen, however, reported that they were denied the right to register as social organizations.[62]

Rule of Law

China's legal system has made significant strides since the Cultural Revolution (1966-1976), when legal and judicial institutions were severely weakened and heavily politicized. According to some analysts, legal reforms may ultimately provide foundations for far-reaching social and political change in China.[63] The state still wields disproportionate power against citizens and legal activists and continues to interpret the law arbitrarily in many cases. However, due to the development of the legal system, the government has been compelled to acknowledge at least some claims regarding violations of legal rights.[64]

---

[58] "Color revolutions" refer to peaceful democratic movements involving mass demonstrations that toppled several post-communist authoritarian governments in former Soviet States such as Georgia, Ukraine, and Kyrgyzstan (2000-05).

[59] Congressional-Executive Commission on China, *Annual Report 2010*, op. cit.

[60] Only foundations can raise funds publicly.

[61] Congressional-Executive Commission on China, *Annual Report 2010*, op. cit.

[62] Jeremy Page, "China Tests New Political Model in Shenzhen," *Wall Street Journal*, October 18, 2010.

[63] Jamie P. Horsley, "The Rule of Law in China: Incremental Progress," *The China Balance Sheet in 2007 and Beyond (Phase II Papers)*, Center for Strategic and International Studies, May 2007.

[64] Paul Mooney, "Beijing Silences 'One-Man Rights Organization,'" *South China Morning Post*, January 27, 2008.

Although some experts suggest that most Chinese still do not place much faith in the nation's courts, other analysts contend that PRC citizens have rising expectations that the state will honor basic legal rights. According to many reports, rising legal awareness and the development of laws have resulted in the growth of legal activity. Chinese citizens increasingly are turning to the courts to assert claims and even to sue public officials. More than 150,000 cases are filed annually against the government, although the rate of success remains low. Some reports point to a trend of modest growth in cases and a more dramatic growth in the number of appeals. PRC lawyers also have begun to file "public interest" cases in growing numbers. Though rarely successful, these cases often draw publicity through the mass media and help to further spread legal consciousness.[65]

China's legal profession has grown quickly from a small base. The country reportedly has roughly 190,000 lawyers, an increase from 110,000 in 2005, or about one for every 7,000 people.[66] This ratio compares to about one lawyer for every 6,000 people in Japan and every 300 in the United States. China's changing legal environment has provided an opening for human rights attorneys, albeit one that is fraught with personal risks. In the past decade, several dozen lawyers in China have made names for themselves by taking on sensitive rights cases against government entities or economic enterprises.[67]

Law firms and lawyers who have pursued prominent human rights or politically sensitive cases have faced a range of troubles, however, including closure of law offices, disbarment, unlawful detention, house arrest, and prison sentences. Many human rights and defense lawyers have been harassed by officials or abducted and beaten by agents of local governments or economic interests. In recent years, the PRC government has stepped up its harassment of many lawyers and law firms that work on prominent human rights or politically sensitive cases. In 2010, the licenses of about a dozen attorneys who had accepted human rights cases were suspended.[68]

In 2008, an amended Law on Lawyers went into effect. Legal reforms included permitting defense lawyers to meet with clients without first seeking permission from judicial authorities; banning police from observing conversations between lawyers and clients; reducing restrictions on access to case files and obtaining evidence; and exempting statements made by lawyers in the courtroom from prosecution. The PRC court system also has implemented programs to strengthen the competence and professionalism of judges and the effectiveness of the judicial system.[69]

Although the new legal provisions provide some protections for attorneys and their clients, defense lawyers remain highly vulnerable, and continue to complain of the "three difficulties of criminal defense"—gaining access to detained clients, reviewing prosecutors' case files, and collecting evidence. Furthermore, pursuant to Article 306 of China's Criminal Law, any defense lawyer accused of fabricating evidence or inducing a witness to change his testimony can be

---

[65] Joseph Kahn, "When Chinese Sue the State, Cases Are Often Smothered," *New York Times*, December 28, 2005; John L. Thornton, "Long Time Coming," *Foreign Affairs*, Vol. 87, no. 1 (January/February 2008).

[66] Glenn Norris and Daniel Ren, "Legal System Less Arbitrary but Still a Work in Progress," *South China Morning Post*, April 4, 2011.

[67] Edward Cody, "China Uses Heavy Hand Even with Gadflies," *Washington Post*, April 9, 2008.

[68] U.S. Department of State, *2010 Human Rights Report*, op. cit.

[69] Benjamin L. Liebman, "China's Courts: Restricted Reform," *The China Quarterly*, no. 191 (September 2007); Eva Pils, "Law: China's Troubled Legal Profession," *Far Eastern Economic Review*," June 6, 2008.

immediately detained, arrested and prosecuted for perjury. Hundreds of lawyers reportedly have been prosecuted under Article 306, although the majority of them have been acquitted.[70]

Despite reforms around the edges, the legal and judicial systems in China remain fundamentally flawed. The Communist Party does not accept the notion of a fully independent judiciary. Although there appears to be an increasing number of cases that are dismissed by PRC courts due to insufficient evidence, the government continues to place a heavy emphasis on establishing the guilt of defendants. There is no adversary system, no presumption of innocence, no protection against double jeopardy, and no law governing the type of evidence that may be introduced. In many instances, police, prosecutors and judges disregard the protections that Chinese law does offer.[71] In criminal and political cases, sentences are decided not by judges but by a court committee named by the Party. The conviction rate for criminal defendants, most of whom did not have legal counsel, was over 99% in 2009.[72]

The Internet

China has the largest number of Internet users in the world, with roughly 450 million people online, including over 300 million mobile Internet users and tens of millions of bloggers.[73] According to one estimate, the number of micro-bloggers in China is expected to reach 100 million in 2011.[74] Although most Internet users in China do not view the medium as a political tool, it has provided many netizens with unprecedented amounts of information, news, and opportunities to express opinions, as well as means to organize protests. While the PRC government generally has managed to prevent politically sensitive information from being disseminated on the Internet or used for political purposes, it has not been able to control all information all the time.

The PRC government employs a variety of methods to control online content and expression, including website (URL) blocking and keyword filtering; regulating Internet service providers, Internet cafes, and university bulletin board systems; registering websites and bloggers; and occasionally arresting of high profile "cyber dissidents."[75] The state routinely blocks many websites, including Radio Free Asia, international human rights websites, and many Taiwan news sites. Nervous about social media as a tool for political organization, the government filters international social networking, blogging and micro-blogging, video, and file sharing sites, such as Facebook, Blogger, Twitter, and YouTube, and offers Chinese versions of them, which it can better control. The government reportedly also has hired thousands of students to express pro-government views on websites, bulletin boards, and chat rooms.[76] Some analysts argue that the PRC government cannot control all Internet content and use, but its selective targeting of users

---

[70] "'Big Stick 306' and China's Contempt for the Law," *New York Times*, May 5, 2011.

[71] Jim Yardley, "Desperate Search for Justice: One Man vs. China," *New York Times*, November 12, 2005.

[72] U.S. Department of State, *2010 Human Rights Report*, op. cit.

[73] *27th Statistical Report on Internet Development in China*, China Internet Network Information Center (CNNIC), January 19, 2011, http://www.cnnic.net.cn/dtygg/dtgg/201101/t20110118_20250.html; "China Has More than 50 Million Web Bloggers," *China Daily*, January 6, 2009; Information Office of the State Council, op. cit.

[74] Zhang Jing, et al. "Micro Revolution Sweeps Nation," *China Daily*, April 22-24, 2011. Micro-blogging sites allow users to exchange ideas through short messages.

[75] Some experts estimate that the PRC government has employed 30,000 "Internet police." "On the Wrong Side of Great Firewall of China," *New Zealand Herald*, November 27, 2007.

[76] David Bandurski, "China's Guerrilla War for the Web," *Far Eastern Economic Review*, July/August 2008.

---

and services creates an undercurrent of fear and promotes self-censorship. In July 2010, major Chinese Internet portals reportedly shut down the blogs of at least 100 prominent scholars, lawyers, and activists. In 2010, according to Reporters Without Borders, 30 reporters and 74 "cyber dissidents" were in prison in China.[77]

Many international English news sites, such as the *WashingtonPost.com*, *NYTimes.com*, *CNN.com*, and Voice of America (English) are generally not jammed, while many Internet users in China circumvent government filtering through the use of proxy servers or virtual private networks using special software. Such methods have enabled many Chinese to access Twitter—dissident artist Ai Weiwei was an avid user before his arrest—despite government censorship of the site.[78] However, following his release form detention on June 22, 2011, Ai was forbidden from posting anything on Twitter for a year.

The state has the capability to block news of events and to partially shut down the Internet. In the Xinjiang Uighur Autonomous Region, following the ethnic unrest that erupted there in July 2009, the government blocked the Internet for ten months. Nonetheless, the sheer volume of information on the Internet means that the state often acts after news is already disseminated, if only fleetingly, online.[79]

Bulletin and comment boards, chat rooms, blogs, and social networking and other outlets have allowed for an unprecedented amount of information and public comment on social issues. Although periodically blocked by the government, blogs have daringly pushed the limits of public discourse. Twitter and domestic micro-blogging sites helped to spread word about Nobel award winner Liu Xiaobo until government censors caught up with the online traffic. One study found that 61% of blogs carried "critical" opinions, including those related to society, government, corporations, and public figures, while 36% of blogs demonstrated "pluralism" or two or more different perspectives.[80] The blogosphere reportedly has been an important forum for discussion of the ecological damage thought to have been caused by the Three Gorges Dam.[81]

Internet and cellular technologies have enhanced the abilities of activists and aggrieved citizens to assemble and to record and publicize social protests and the actions of government officials. In the summer of 2010, the Internet and cell phones helped disgruntled and striking workers throughout China to communicate domestically and internationally, expose human rights abuses, learn from each other's protest strategies, and research relevant labor laws. The threat of public exposure and condemnation reportedly has compelled some government officials to conduct affairs more openly. The PRC government has referred positively to the "Internet's role in supervision." One report lists a growing number of cases in which large-scale "Internet protests" have resulted in the punishment of errant officials or retractions of policies.[82] Several government

---

[77] U.S. Department of State, *2010 Human Rights Report*, op. cit.

[78] David Pierson, "Scaling the Great Firewall; More of China's Web Users Find Ways Around Aggressive Censorship," *Los Angeles Times*, January 16, 2010.

[79] Loretta Chao and Jason Dean, "Analysis: China is Losing a War over Internet," *Wall Street Journal*, December 31, 2009.

[80] Rebecca MacKinnon, "Flatter World and Thicker Walls? Blogs, Censorship and Civic Discourse in China," *Public Choice*, Vol. 134 (January 2008).

[81] William Wan, "Amid Severe Drought, Chinese Government Admits Mistakes with Three Gorges Dam," *Washington Post*, June 4, 2011.

[82] Information Office of the State Council, op. cit.; Yanqi Tong and Shaohua Lei, "Creating Public Opinion Pressure in China: Large-Scale Internet Protest," *East Asian Institute (Singapore) Background Brief No. 534*, June 17, 2010.

departments have set up "informant websites" to facilitate the reporting of corrupt or negligent officials. Furthermore, official news outlets have become much quicker to report on news events, albeit the government's version of the stories, in order to respond to news that has been spread independently on the Internet.

The PRC government has displayed a growing nervousness about the Internet's influence on Chinese society and politics, although it has attempted to enact and enforce restrictions judiciously and selectively, and to induce self-censorship, in order to avoid provoking an uproar among China's online and foreign business communities. In recent years, the government has attempted to impose greater surveillance upon Internet users. Although this effort ostensibly has focused upon curtailing Internet pornography and other illegal content, it also has had a chilling effect on political content and discourse. New guidelines include requiring users to provide their real names and official identification numbers when they post online comments or patronize Internet cafes and public libraries. Applicants for ".cn" domain names now must provide a color headshot photo as well as other forms of personal identification.

Internet cafes are obligated to install software to track online activity, although they reportedly have been somewhat lax regarding obtaining personal information.[83] The Ministry of Industry and Information Technology has increased pressure on Internet service providers to monitor the content and online activities of individuals and webmasters, including the transfer of state secrets.[84] In May 2011, the PRC government created a new central agency, the State Internet Information Office, to better coordinate the myriad agencies that oversee the Internet in China.

The Internet has proven to be less of a political factor than many observers had expected or hoped. Users who mine the Internet for political information reportedly make up a small minority, and between 2% and 8% of Internet users in China access proxy servers to get around government-erected firewalls.[85] For many of China's educated elite who frequent English-language sites, the availability of foreign news to a minority of Chinese citizens is not nearly as critical as the ability to seek political change on the basis of such information. Such ability remains substantially curtailed. Furthermore, some analysts suggest that the limited amount of Internet freedom in China defuses political activism by allowing people to vent their opinions online.[86] Finally, many Chinese Internet users support the idea of censorship, particularly the government's efforts to ban online pornography, gambling, illegal commerce, phishing, and spam.[87] Nonetheless, the State Department reported that in the past year, a small community of dissidents and political activists "continued to use the Internet to advocate and call attention to political causes such as prisoner advocacy, political reform, ethnic discrimination, corruption, and foreign policy concerns."[88]

---

[83] U.S. Department of State, *2010 Human Rights Report*, op. cit.

[84] Gillian Wong, "China Set to Tighten State-Secrets Law Forcing Internet Firms to Inform on Users," *Washington Post*, April 28, 2010.

[85] Rebecca MacKinnon, "Bloggers and Censors: Chinese Media in the Internet Age," *China Studies Center*, May 18, 2007; John Pomfret, "U.S. Risks Ire with Decision to Fund Software Maker Tied to Falun Gong," *Washington Post*, May 12, 2010.

[86] Andrew Jacobs, "China's Web Wild Card: Economic Downturn Crisis a Threat to Censors' Tight Control," *International Herald Tribune*, February 6, 2009.

[87] Rebecca MacKinnon, "Is Web 2.0 a Wash for Free Speech in China?" *RConversation*, http://rconversation.blogs.com.

[88] U.S. Department of State, *2010 Human Rights Report*, op. cit.

Google in China

In January 2010, Google, at the time the second-most popular search engine in the PRC after China's *Baidu,* and reportedly the least censored, claimed that Chinese hackers had attacked its Gmail service and corporate network as well as the computer systems of many other large U.S. corporations in the PRC.[89] Google's chief legal officer announced that the company would no longer censor results on Google.cn, even if that meant having to shut down its search engine, and potentially its offices, in China. The PRC government accused Google of violating a written promise to filter its search engine and abide by Chinese laws, after the company began re-routing users automatically to its uncensored Hong Kong site.

In July 2010, China renewed Google's license, after the company set up a link on its landing page to its Hong Kong search engine, rather than continuing its practice of automatically re-directing users to the Hong Kong site. Although Google's Hong Kong search engine is not censored, China can block sites or search results it deems undesirable. Some analysts regarded this as a compromise—Google can still be accessed in China (through Hong Kong), but there is no direct link to the Hong Kong site. Google's share of China's search-engine market fell to 19.6% in the fourth quarter of 2010 from 30% a year earlier, according to research company Analysys International. Baidu's market share rose to 75.5% from 58% at the end of 2009.[90] In June 2011, Google claimed that hackers likely originating in China attempted to access hundreds of Gmail accounts, including those of U.S. government officials. The PRC government denied involvement in both the 2009 and 2011 hacking incidents.

The Media

The state directly controls the largest mass media outlets, pressures other media enterprises regarding major or sensitive stories, and imposes severe measures against its critics. However, overall, the PRC government exercises less control over news and information than it did a decade ago, and in the past year, the "range of permissible public discourse continued to expand, with significant exceptions."[91] One scholar characterizes state control of the media as evolving from one of "omnipresence to selective enforcement."[92] The greater volume and variety of news reporting has not translated into fundamental advances in freedom of expression, but nor have new regulations and policies affecting journalists and other critical voices significantly curbed the flow of information, thanks in large part to the Internet. In some cases, the government has supported journalistic efforts to expose official corruption and incompetence, particularly at the local level. The press has become more open about issues related to food safety, highlighted the challenges facing social organizations, lawyers, petitioners, and Internet users, and documented and broached sensitive issues, such as social unrest, abuses of detainees, and the network of black jails.[93]

---

[89] Steven Mufson, "China Faces Backlash from 'Netizens' if Google Leaves," *Washington Post,* January 13, 2010.

[90] Mark Lee, "Google Loses China Search-Engine Market Share, Researcher Says," *Bloomberg.com,* January 18, 2011.

[91] U.S. Department of State, *2010 Human Rights Report,* op. cit.

[92] Hongying Wang and Xueyi Chen, "Globalization and the Changing State-Media Relations in China," Paper Prepared for Presentation at the 2008 Annual Conference of the American Political Science Association, August 38-31, 2008.

[93] Ariana Eunjung Cha, "Public Anger over Milk Scandal Forces China's Hand," *Washington Post,* September 19, 2008; "China Gives Press More Freedom for Food Safety," *Associated Press,* May 16, 2011; Congressional-Executive Commission on China, *Annual Report 2010,* op. cit.

Increasingly commercialized media outlets negotiate a delicate balance between responding to growing public demands for information and remaining within the bounds of what authorities will allow and advertisers will support. Under the economic reform policies of the past two decades, a burgeoning private media industry has developed, pushing the limits of social, cultural and, to a small extent, political content. Traditional state media have had to provide more probing and provocative fare in order to attract readers, stay competitive, and respond to news and public opinion appearing on the Internet. The chief editor of a major official publication explained that he is pressured by both the market and his Communist Party bosses: "I live between them. But the market has a bigger and bigger influence."[94] However, another study suggests that reporting that is too provocative may risk not only government sanction but also a loss of advertising revenue.[95]

The tug-of-war between the state's attempts to maintain social and political control, on the one hand, and, on the other hand, society's demand for news and information, is likely to continue. China's leaders still view the ultimate duty of reporters and the mass media as serving the state. In 2010, new requirements for journalists included knowledge of "Communist Party journalism and Marxist views of news."[96] The state intimidates journalists and authors through criminal prosecution and civil lawsuits, as well as violence, detention, and other forms of harassment.[97] Newspaper editors continue to face possible punishment for publishing major stories of controversy. In March 2010, the top editor of the independent *Economic Observer* was dismissed after sponsoring an editorial published in 13 newspapers, including his own, that was critical of China's household registration system (*hukou*), which restricts migration within the country.

Growing numbers of Internet users reportedly are chafing against information controls and expressing such frustrations online.[98] Journalists are increasingly willing to speak out in support of their right to report stories, if not "press freedom" per se, particularly regarding corporate scandals and, occasionally, local corruption. In one survey, while 40% of journalists in a sample believed that the news media should play a watchdog role, only 19% believed that the their organization emphasized this function.[99] In October 2010, a group of prominent Party elders posted an open letter online calling for the end to restrictions on speech and the press.[100]

Religious Freedom

The extent of religious freedom and activity in China varies widely by region and jurisdiction. Hundreds of millions of Chinese openly practice one of five officially recognized religions (Buddhism, Protestantism, Roman Catholicism, Daoism, and Islam) and religious organizations are playing growing roles in providing social and charitable services. The PRC Constitution protects "normal" religious activities and those that do not "disrupt public order, impair the health

---

[94] Keith B. Richburg, "Chinese Editors, and a Web Site, Detail Censors' Hidden Hand," *Washington Post*, April 12, 2011.

[95] Christopher Walker and Sarah Cook, "China's Commercialization of Censorship," *Far Eastern Economic Review*, May 2, 2009.

[96] Congressional-Executive Commission on China, *Annual Report 2010*, op. cit.

[97] U.S. Department of State, *2010 Human Rights Report*, op. cit.

[98] Howard W. French, "Great Firewall of China Faces Online Rebels," *New York Times*, February 4, 2008.

[99] Madeline Earp, "In China, A Debate on Press Rights," *Committee to Protect Journalists*, October 10, 2010; Fen Lin, "A Survey Report on Chinese Journalists in China," *The China Quarterly*, No. 202, 2010.

[100] Christopher Bodeen, "Chinese Communist Elders Issue Free Speech Appeal," *Yahoo! News*, October 13, 2010.

of citizens or interfere with the educational system of the state." The government officially disapproves of religious groups that are not incorporated into official bodies. Although in many localities, unsanctioned religious congregations receive little state interference, they still are vulnerable to arbitrary restrictions and possible shutdown by authorities. The PRC government imposes especially draconian policies and measures upon many unofficial Christian churches, Tibetan Buddhists, Uighur Muslims, and Falun Gong practitioners, largely due to the potential for these groups to become independent social forces and cultivate foreign support. The Department of State has identified China as a "country of particular concern" (CPC) for "particularly severe violations of religious freedom" for 12 consecutive years (2000-2011).[101]

Chinese Christians

Despite restrictions, Christian worship has continued to grow. According to some estimates, roughly 30 million Chinese Christians worship in state-sanctioned, "official" churches, while over 70 million Chinese practice their faith in unregistered, mostly Protestant congregations. Unofficial churches, or "house churches," lack legal protections and remain highly vulnerable to human rights abuses by local officials. In some areas, particularly in the more affluent southeastern provinces, many unofficial congregations reportedly experience little state interference. In other areas, however, such groups often face harassment by government authorities, their leaders have been beaten, detained, and imprisoned, and their properties have been destroyed.

Many problems involving house churches stem from ambiguities over registration requirements and distrust between unofficial congregations and the State Administration for Religious Affairs. Many Chinese Protestants have rejected the official church, known as the Three Self Patriotic Movement, for political or theological reasons, while some house churches claim that their attempts to apply for official status have been rejected by the local religious affairs bureau.[102] In some cases, government officials have claimed that foreign missionaries have discouraged unofficial churches from registering with the state.[103] Catholics in China are divided between those who follow the Pope and those who belong to the official Chinese Catholic Patriotic Association, which does not recognize the Pope's authority. Beijing and the Vatican have long been at odds regarding which side has the authority to appoint bishops, although most Chinese bishops have received approval from both Beijing and the Holy See.

According to ChinaAid, an organization that monitors human rights abuses against Christians in China, the persecution of Christians has worsened for five consecutive years, and the number of Christians arrested soared by nearly 43% (from 389 to 556 people), between 2009 and 2010.[104] In the past year, PRC authorities reportedly temporarily detained over 500 members of unofficial churches and stepped up efforts to prevent unsanctioned congregations from worshipping. At least 40 unregistered Chinese bishops reportedly are under surveillance, in hiding, in detention,

---

[101] This designation has subjected the PRC to U.S. sanctions pursuant to the International Religious Freedom Act of 1998 (P.L. 105-292), including a ban on the U.S. export of crime control and detection instruments and equipment to China.

[102] "Three Self" refers to self-governance, self-support, and self-propagation, or independence from foreign missionary and other religious groups and influences.

[103] Brookings Institution, "Religion in China: Perspectives from Chinese Religious Leaders," September 11, 2008.

[104] "Government Persecution of Church in China Worsens for Fifth Straight Year," *China Aid Association*, April 1, 2011.

confined to their homes, or have disappeared.[105] Beijing authorities refused to allow the 1,000-member Shouwang Protestant church, one of the largest unofficial congregations in China, to occupy the premises that it purchased in 2009, and in April 2011 evicted the congregation from its rented space. The government has placed some Shouwang church leaders under house arrest and detained members who have attempted to gather outside on consecutive Sundays.[106]

Tibet

Many Tibetans have long resented PRC political controls and intrusions into their religious beliefs and practices. Other sources of grievance for Tibetans include the loss of their traditional culture and language, the domination of the local economy by Han Chinese (the majority ethnic group in China), limitations on international contacts, and the adverse environmental effects of Beijing's development projects in the region. Han Chinese form a minority in the Tibet Autonomous Region (TAR), about 8% of the total population of roughly 3 million people, but constitute about half of the population of Lhasa, the Tibetan capital.[107] Many Han Chinese believe that the PRC government has brought positive economic and social development to the region.

On March 11, 2008, the 49th anniversary of the 1959 Tibetan uprising against Chinese rule, 300 Buddhist monks demonstrated peacefully to demand the release of Tibetan prisoners of conscience. These demonstrations sparked others by monks and ordinary Tibetans demanding independence from China or greater autonomy, one of the most sensitive political issues for Beijing. On March 15, demonstrations in Lhasa turned violent as Tibetan protesters confronted PRC police and burned Han shops and property. Other Tibetan protests erupted in Tibetan areas of neighboring Gansu, Qinghai, and Sichuan provinces. Official PRC news sources, emphasizing Han Chinese casualties, reported that 19 persons died in the riots. The government blamed the Dalai Lama, the exiled Tibetan spiritual leader, for instigating the riots and labeled his followers "separatists." From India, where he is based, the Dalai Lama denied involvement and appealed to both the Chinese government and his followers to refrain from violence.

In the aftermath of the unrest, an estimated 100 to 218 persons were killed in Tibet and other Tibetan areas, likely in conflicts with PRC security forces, and 76 people, mostly Tibetans, were sentenced to prison terms ranging from three years to life.[108] In 2010, there reportedly were 824 known Tibetan prisoners of conscience.[109] The government also expanded and intensified "patriotic education" campaigns in monasteries and nunneries.

China's leaders reportedly renewed efforts to spur economic development in Tibet, provide greater economic opportunities for Tibetans, and improve social services, but have displayed little, if any, flexibility on the questions of greater autonomy and religious freedom. However,

---

[105] Congressional-Executive Commission on China, *Annual Report 2010*, op. cit.

[106] Arrest of Shouwang Christians and Other Believers Relentless, *Asia News*, June 6, 2011, http://www.chinaaid.org/2011/06/arrest-of-shouwang-christians-and-other.html.

[107] Base upon PRC data. "Tibet's Population Tops 3 Million; 90% Are Tibetans," *Xinhua*, May 4, 2011. Some observers believe that the number of Han Chinese in Tibet is far higher.

[108] *2010 Human Rights Report*, op. cit.

[109] Congressional-Executive Commission on China, *Annual Report 2010*, op. cit.

some Chinese scholars and lower level officials reportedly have continued to criticize the effectiveness of government policies.[110]

The eighth round of dialogue between Beijing and envoys of the Dalai Lama since 2002, which took place in November 2008, failed to bring about any fundamental progress on the issue of greater autonomy for Tibet. The ninth round took place in January 2010, with the Dalai Lama's representatives pledging respect for the authority of the Chinese central government, but continuing to push for "genuine autonomy" for the Tibetan people within China. Both sides indicated that the meetings produced no breakthroughs.

The government clampdown on the Kirti Tibetan monastery in Sichuan province reportedly continues following unrest there earlier in the year. In April 2011, PRC security forces sealed off the monastery and cultural center after a monk there set himself on fire in protest against government policies toward Tibetans. Police reportedly detained 300 monks and forcefully dispersed local Tibetans who attempted to prevent them from being taken into custody, resulting in the deaths of two elderly people.[111]

In April 2011, Tibetan exiles in India elected a Harvard academic, Lobsang Sangay, as their new prime minister. He is expected to assume some of the political duties of the Dalai Lama, who announced his retirement from his political role in March 2011, although the Dalai Lama's representatives will continue to represent the Tibetan exiles in the dialogue with Beijing. The Chinese government has vowed not to conduct any talks with the new prime minister and his government, arguing that they represent an illegal organization.

U.S. Policy Toward Tibet

The Tibetan Policy Act of 2002 (P.L. 107-228) directs the Executive Branch to encourage the PRC government to enter into a dialogue with the Dalai Lama or his representatives, call for the release of Tibetan political and religious prisoners in China, support economic development, cultural preservation, environmental sustainability, and other objectives in Tibet, and carry out other activities to "support the aspirations of the Tibetan people to safeguard their distinct identity."[112] In July 2011, President Obama met with the Dalai Lama at the White House, despite strong objections from Beijing. The President emphasized the importance of the human rights of Tibetans in China as well as their unique religious, cultural, and linguistic traditions. He stressed that Tibet is a part of China, praised the Dalai Lama's commitment to nonviolence and his "Middle Way" approach, and encouraged dialogue between the Dalai Lama's representatives and Beijing, while also emphasizing the importance of U.S.-China cooperation.

Uighur Muslims

According to some experts, most Muslim communities in the western Ningxia Hui Autonomous Region, and Gansu, Qinghai, and Yunnan Provinces coexist relatively peacefully with non-Muslims and experience little conflict with local authorities.[113] However, social and political tensions and harsh religious policies have long plagued China's far northwestern Xinjiang Uighur Autonomous Region (XUAR), which is home to 8.5 million Uighur Muslims, a Turkic ethnic

---

[110] Ibid.

[111] "Tibetan Government in Exile 'Deeply Concerned' About China Crackdown on Monastery," *VOA News*, April 23, 2011.

[112] For further information, see CRS Report R41108, *U.S.-China Relations: Policy Issues*, by Susan V. Lawrence and Thomas Lum.

[113] Ben Blanchard, "Religion, Politics Mix Awkwardly for China's Muslims," *Washington Post*, May 26, 2006.

group.[114] Once the predominant group in the region, they now constitute an estimated 40% of its population as many Han Chinese have migrated there, particularly to the capital, Urumqi.[115] Uighurs and human rights groups have complained of PRC religious policies that restrict the training and role of imams, the celebration of Ramadan, and participation in the hajj. Uighur children are forbidden from entering mosques and government workers and teachers are not allowed to openly practice Islam. Other grievances include a loss of ethnic identity, economic discrimination, and a lack of democracy. Government efforts to demolish the old city of Kashgar, ostensibly to build new housing and improve public safety, have angered many Uighurs. Many long time Kashgar residents, who say they have not been adequately consulted on the redevelopment plans, argue that the policy is aimed at controlling the local population. Many Han Chinese agree with government assertions that PRC policies have benefitted Uighurs, that Muslims receive preferential treatment due to special policies toward minority groups, and that firm policies are necessary to prevent terrorism.

The Chinese government fears not only Uighur demands for greater religious freedom but also Uighurs' links to Central Asian countries and foreign Islamic organizations. The Chinese government claims that the East Turkestan Islamic Movement (ETIM), a Uighur organization that advocates the creation of an independent Uighur Islamic state, has been responsible for small-scale terrorist attacks in China and has ties to Al Qaeda. ETIM is on the United States' and United Nations' lists of terrorist organizations.[116] Due to perceived national security-related concerns, the PRC government has imposed stern constraints on the religious and cultural practices of Uighurs in Xinjiang, often conflating them with subversive activities or the "three evils of religious extremism, splittism, and terrorism."

On July 5, 2009, an estimated several hundred to a few thousand Uighur demonstrators gathered peacefully in Urumqi to demand that PRC authorities prosecute those responsible for the deaths of two Uighur men involved in a brawl between Han and Uighur factory workers in Guangdong province. Paramilitary police reportedly attacked the demonstrators after they refused to disperse, which eventually provoked a riot and acts of violence against government property, Han residents, and Han shops. In response, bands of Han Chinese sought retribution against Uighurs.

The Chinese government blamed Uighur "separatists" and exile groups for planning the riots, particularly the World Uygur Congress led by exiled Uighur leader and former PRC political prisoner Rebiya Kadeer.[117] The Xinjiang government reported nearly 200 deaths, about two-thirds of them Han, and 1,700 people injured. The State Department reported that at the end of 2010, 26 people had been sentenced to death and nine received suspended death sentences. Of these individuals, three were Han and the rest Uighur.[118]

Following the July 2009 unrest, the government further restricted speech, assembly, religious activity, information, and international communication in Uighur areas, including blocking

---

[114] Estimates of China's Muslim population range from 20 million to 30 million people.

[115] Preeti Bhattacharji, "Uighurs and China's Xinjiang Region," *Council on Foreign Relations Backgrounder*, July 6, 2009.

[116] For further information, see CRS Report RL33001, *U.S.-China Counterterrorism Cooperation: Issues for U.S. Policy*, by Shirley A. Kan.

[117] Kadeer's sons, Alim Abdireyim, Kahar Abdureyim, and Ablikim Abdireyim, are serving jail sentences for tax evasion and "engaging in secessionist activities."

[118] U.S. Department of State, *2010 Human Rights Report*, op. cit.

Internet access for ten months. The Xinjiang government also has intensified the use of Mandarin in schools. Over 1,000 people in Xinjiang, including Uighur journalists and webmasters who had published sensitive information, reportedly have been arrested in the past two years on charges related to state security.[119] The whereabouts of 20 Uighur asylum seekers repatriated from Cambodia to China remained unknown at the end of 2010.[120] Government efforts to address social instability in Xinjiang have focused upon economic development and cultural preservation, rather than religious and political freedoms.[121]

Falun Gong

Falun Gong combines an exercise regimen with meditation, moral values, and spiritual beliefs. The practice and beliefs are derived from *qigong*, a set of movements said to stimulate the flow of *qi*— vital energies or "life forces"—throughout the body, and Buddhist and Daoist concepts. The spiritual exercise reportedly gained tens of millions of adherents across China in the late 1990s. On April 25, 1999, thousands of practitioners gathered in Beijing to protest the government's growing restrictions on their activities. Following a crackdown that began in the summer of 1999 and deepened in intensity over a period of roughly two years, the group, which the government labeled a dangerous or "evil" cult, ceased to practice or demonstrate in the open. Nonetheless, government efforts to suppress the group continued. Overseas Falun Gong organizations reported that the government intensified its persecution of Falun Gong during the period of the 2008 Olympics and 2009 Shanghai World Expo.[122] Many practitioners who did not renounce their beliefs reportedly were held in reeducation through labor camps and subjected to torture and other abuses.[123]

According to the Congressional-Executive Commission on China, citing CCP documents, the PRC government has launched a three-year campaign (2010-2012) to "transform" Falun Gong adherents, calling upon local governments, Party organizations, businesses, and individuals to step up efforts to reeducate practitioners and persuade or compel them to denounce their beliefs. Gao Zhisheng, a rights lawyer who had defended Falun Gong adherents, was apprehended by PRC police in 2009 and remains missing. Another lawyer who had defended Falun Gong practitioners, Wang Yonghang, was sentenced to seven years in prison on the charge of "using a cult organization to undermine the implementation of the law."[124]

According to some sources, Falun Gong adherents constitute an estimated two-thirds of all prisoners and detainees of conscience in China, or roughly 15,000 people. Since 1999, over 6,000 Falun Gong adherents reportedly have served time in prison. During the initial crackdown on the group, the proportion of Falun Gong adherents in reeducation through labor camps may have been as high as one-quarter to one-half of all RTL inmates, or 70,000 to 125,000 people. Estimates of the number of those who died in state custody have ranged from several hundred to a

---

[119] U.S. Commission on International Religious Freedom, *Annual Report 2011*, May 2011, citing the State Department.

[120] U.S. Department of State, *2010 Human Rights Report*, op. cit.

[121] "Efforts to Boost 'Leapfrog' Development in Xinjiang," *Xinhua*, July 5, 2010.

[122] Andrew Jacobs, "China Still Presses Crusade Against Falun Gong," *New York Times*, April 28, 2009.

[123] U.S. Department of State, *2010 Human Rights Report*, op. cit.

[124] "Communist Party Calls for Increased Efforts to 'Transform' Falun Gong Practitioners as Part of Three-Year Campaign," *Congressional-Executive Commission on China*, March 22, 2011; Congressional-Executive Commission on China, *Annual Report 2010*, op. cit.

few thousand. Falun Gong groups claim to have documented nearly 3,500 deaths in custody between 1999 and 2011, although they assert that the number of undocumented cases could be much higher. These deaths have been concentrated in seven provinces—Heilongjiang, Hebei, Liaoning, Jilin, Shandong, Sichuan, and Hubei.[125]

Social Variables Affecting Human Rights

Social Unrest

Daily incidences of social unrest in China highlight the rising rights consciousness of PRC citizens, widening disparities of income and power stemming from rapid economic change, and the inability of China's political institutions and legal system to adequately resolve social grievances. The government has applied a carrot-and-stick approach toward disgruntled social groups, often sympathizing with them and pressuring local authorities to give in to some demands, while arresting protest leaders, intimidating activists, and thwarting linkages among them. The developing rights awareness of many Chinese citizens, combined with small but passionate networks of lawyers, journalists, and activists, suggests that social pressures for advancing human rights are likely to continue.

In the past decade, major types of social unrest have included the following: state-owned enterprise workers demonstrating against layoffs; migrant laborers protesting lack of pay; farmers objecting to unfair taxation and usurious fees, confiscation of land for development projects, and loss of agricultural land due to environmental degradation; and homeowners opposing forcible evictions related to urban development. In cases of land confiscation and home evictions, much popular anger has been directed at collusive deals between local officials and private investors and the lack of fair compensation to ordinary citizens.

Relatively new sources of social unrest have included farmers claiming ownership of land; the closing of thousands of factories due to climbing labor and energy costs and the rising value of the Chinese currency; consumer price inflation; and coercive enforcement of the one-child policy.[126] Another potential source of unrest is the high unemployment rate among recent college graduates in China, which is estimated to be around 26%.[127] Resentment toward government restrictions of ethnic and religious practices, anger against the economic dominance of Han Chinese, and the lack of political participation remain deep-seated problems in Tibet and Xinjiang. In May 2011, student demonstrations broke out in Inner Mongolia over the deaths of two Mongolians involved in earlier protests.[128]

So far, numerous but scattered social protests have not evolved into broad-based political movements. Rather than perceiving local problems in national, political terms, aggrieved citizens

---

[125] U.S. Department of State, *2009 Human Rights Report: China*, March 11, 2010; Dui Hua Foundation estimates; "Overview of Death Cases of Falun Gong Practitioners Due to Persecution," *ClearWisdom.net*, May 18, 2011, http://www.clearwisdom.net/html/articles/2011/5/18/125337p.html.

[126] Bill Powell, "China's At-Risk Factories," *Time*, April 28, 2008; Edward Cody, "Farmers Rise in Challenge to Chinese Land Policy," *Washington Post*, January 14, 2008.

[127] Michael Wei, "East Meets West at Hamburger University," *Bloomberg Businessweek*, January 31-February 6, 2011.

[128] "China's Inner Mongolia Region under Heavy Security Following Ethnic Protests," *Washington Post*, May 29, 2011; "No Pastoral Idyll," *The Economist*, June 2, 2011.

generally have demonstrated against local officials and enterprise managers for not acting in accordance with the law, while often viewing central government leaders as well-intentioned. When protest groups have attempted to join forces, China's leaders have quashed such linkages.

Although generally supportive of the status quo, the urban middle class has begun to engage in narrowly targeted demonstrations. The growing involvement of the middle class is potentially significant, given their effectiveness in organizing and articulating interests and their importance to the central government's legitimacy. However, the middle class has demonstrated a reluctance to identify and join forces with other social strata.

The Middle Class

Many political theorists and policy makers have argued that the growth of the middle and entrepreneurial classes in developing market economies creates pressures for democracy. According to these hypotheses, demands for rights and democracy stem from desires to protect economic interests and political influence, a growing sense of entitlement, and confidence in their capacity to affect or participate in decision-making. However, some studies suggest that social groups in China that have benefitted from economic reforms value incremental over dramatic or potentially disruptive political change. Many members of China's rising middle class, who are predominantly educated city dwellers, have displayed either a lack of interest in politics or a preference for political stability rather than rapid reform. They have been careful not to jeopardize their hard-won economic gains, and have expressed some fear of grassroots democracy.[129]

Findings based upon surveys of urban Chinese indicate that the middle class is assertive about clean and responsive government and politically aware but also dependent upon the state for its economic well-being and somewhat politically conservative. According to one survey, urban residents can be critical of the state regarding economic issues, but they are not prone to agitate for democracy if they perceive their economic needs as being served. Although members of the China's middle class support civil liberties, they are not especially interested in exercising political rights through multi-party elections. They are less inclined than other classes to participate in demonstrations and more inclined to accept government decision-making. However, they are supportive of existing, somewhat informal processes of contacting and petitioning local officials.[130]

According to recent studies conducted by a government think tank, the Chinese Academy of Social Sciences, the Chinese middle class, which comprises nearly 25% of the population according to some estimates, is especially critical of political corruption and crony capitalism which affect their economic opportunities. The middle class wants access to information, to feel that its voice is being heard, and opportunities to engage in social action. But it also is defensive about China's achievements and resentful of international criticism.[131] Similarly, many Chinese youth reportedly are liberal in outlook and assertive regarding their rights, but also are career-

---

[129] See Willy Wo-Lap Lam, *Chinese Politics in the Hu Jintao Era*, M.E. Sharpe: Armonk, NY, 2006.

[130] Jie Chen, "Attitudes toward Democracy and the Behavior of China's Middle Class," in Cheng Li, ed. *China's Emerging Middle Class*, Washington: Brookings Institution Press, 2010.

[131] Brookings Institution, China's Emerging Middle Class: Beyond Economic Transformation, December 14, 2010.

---

oriented, politically pragmatic, and fiercely patriotic. Although Chinese youth often are critical of their own government, many are quick to reject Western criticism of their country.[132]

Rather than asserting its independence from the state, China's business sector has remained heavily dependent upon it. Many entrepreneurs seek close relations with government agencies that ensure their survival. The Chinese Communist Party, in turn, has welcomed business persons into the Party. The PRC government wields influence over the private sector not only through its authority over business transactions, but also through its controls over many other areas of the economy, such as finance and property. Furthermore, the weakness of China's legal system means that many business persons must seek relations with government officials in order to protect their assets or enforce contracts. According to several studies, private entrepreneurs favor strengthening the legal system and support long-term political reform, but also value social stability and are satisfied with the current, slow pace of change.[133]

U.S. Efforts to Advance Human Rights in China

In the past two decades, successive U.S. administrations have developed a comprehensive array of tactics and programs aimed toward promoting democracy, human rights, and the rule of law in China, but their effects have been felt primarily along the margins of the PRC political system. The U.S. government has pressured China from without through monitoring and openly criticizing the country's human rights record and calling upon the PRC leadership to honor the rights guaranteed in its constitution, bring its policies in line with international standards, release prisoners of conscience, and undertake political reforms. Washington also has supported programs within China that aim to strengthen the rule of law, civil society, government accountability, and labor rights. It has supported U.S.-based NGOs and Internet companies that monitor human rights conditions in China and help enable Chinese Internet users to access Voice of America, Radio Free Asia, and other blocked websites.

Some experts argue that diplomatic and economic engagement with China have failed to set any real political change in motion. In this context, some observers believe, U.S. efforts to promote democracy and human rights have been largely ineffectual. Many policy makers suggest that tangible improvements in PRC human rights policies should be a condition for full diplomatic and economic relations with China as well as cooperation on other issues. Other observers counter that Washington has little direct leverage on China's internal policies, and that U.S. engagement and human rights efforts have helped to set conditions in place that are conducive for progress. They contend that sanctions and linking bilateral cooperation to PRC improvements in human rights have not been very effective.[134]

---

[132] Teresa Wright, "Disincentives for Democratic Change in China," *East-West Center Asia Pacific Issues*, No. 82, February 2007; Brookings Institution, "Understanding China's 'Angry Youth': What Does the Future Hold?" April 29, 2009.

[133] Bruce J. Dickson, "Integrating Wealth and Power in China: The Communist Party's Embrace of the Private Sector," *The China Quarterly*, no. 192, December 2007; Kellee S. Tsai, "China's Complicit Capitalists," *Far Eastern Economic Review*, January/February 2008; Bruce J. Dickson and Jie Chen, "Engaging the State: Political Activities of Private Entrepreneurs in China," Paper Prepared for Presentation at the 2008 Annual Conference of the American Political Science Association, August 38-31, 2008.

[134] See David M. Lampton, "'The China Fantasy,' Fantasy," *The China Quarterly*, No. 191 (September 2007); James Mann, "Rejoinder to David M. Lampton," *The China Quarterly*, No. 191 (September 2007); "Not So Obvious: The Secretary Of State Underestimates The Power Of Her Words," *Washington Post*, February 2009; "A Bow to Reality, (continued...)

Selected Policy Tools

Many U.S. experts and policy makers have disagreed over the best policy approaches, priorities, and methods to apply toward promoting democracy and human rights in China. Differing U.S. goals include effecting fundamental political change in China, on the one hand, and supporting incremental progress, on the other. Possible approaches range from placing human rights conditions upon the bilateral relationship to inducing change through bilateral and international engagement. Policy tools include private discussions; sanctions; open criticism of PRC human rights policies; coordinating international pressure; support of and contact with dissidents; bilateral dialogue; human rights, democracy, and related programs in the PRC; promoting Internet freedom; public diplomacy efforts; and monitoring and highlighting human rights abuses.

Sanctions

Many U.S. sanctions on the PRC in response to the Tiananmen military crackdown in 1989 remain in effect, including some foreign aid-related restrictions, such as required "no" votes or abstentions by U.S. representatives to international financial institutions regarding loans to China (except those that meet basic human needs).[135] Since 2004, Congress has required that U.S. representatives to international financial institutions support projects in Tibet only if they do not encourage the migration and settlement of non-Tibetans into Tibet or the transfer of Tibetan-owned properties to non-Tibetans.[136] Foreign operations appropriations measures have prohibited assistance to the United Nations Population Fund from being used to support related programs in China.[137]

Openly Criticizing China

Some analysts argue that the U.S. government should take principled stands against China's human rights abuses more frequently, openly, and forcefully, while others believe that such methods can undermine human rights efforts. Many prominent dissidents and former prisoners of conscience have claimed that international pressure or attention protected them from harsher treatment by PRC authorities. While some members of civil society groups have welcomed a more assertive U.S. human rights policy, others have cautioned that the Chinese government often has restricted their activities when they were viewed as tied to foreign democracy efforts.

In some cases, the PRC government has made small concessions in order to help reduce or avoid open U.S. or global criticism. Some analysts suggested that Beijing's agreement to restart the U.S.-PRC human rights dialogue in 2008 was linked to the U.S. State Department's decision not to include China in a list of "worst human rights violators." In other cases, the Chinese leadership

(...continued)

Not China," *USA Today*, February 27, 2009; Thomas J. Christensen, "Shaping the Choices of a Rising China: Recent Lessons for the Obama Administration," *The Washington Quarterly*, July 2009; William F. Schulz, "Strategic Persistence: How the United States Can Help Improve Human Rights in China," *Center for American Progress*, January 2009.

[135] See CRS Report RL31910, *China: Economic Sanctions*, by Dianne E. Rennack.

[136] See Consolidated Appropriations Act, 2004 (P.L. 108-199, Sec. 558) and Consolidated Appropriations Act, 2010 (P.L. 111-117, Sec. 7071(a)(1)).

[137] Consolidated Appropriations Act, 2010 (P.L. 111-117, Sec. 7078(c)). For further information, see CRS Report RL32703, *The U.N. Population Fund: Background and the U.S. Funding Debate*, by Luisa Blanchfield.

has reacted angrily or responded in a "tit for tat" manner when the U.S. government publicly denounced its human rights policies, as when Beijing suspended the dialogue in 2004 after the Bush Administration sponsored an unsuccessful U.N. resolution criticizing China's human rights record.[138]

Congressional Actions

Congressional actions publicizing China's human rights violations have included numerous resolutions, bills, hearings, and visits to the PRC. Various resolutions have called attention to the imprisonment and detention of political, religious, and minority figures; persecution of Tibetans, Uighurs, and Falun Gong adherents; censorship of the Internet and other mass media; coercive abortions; and China's deportation of North Korean refugees. Some bills have aimed to restrict U.S.-China trade on the basis of PRC human rights abuses. In July 2008, Representatives Chris Smith and Frank Wolf traveled to Beijing in an effort to discuss human rights issues with PRC and U.S. officials. They also attempted to meet with several Chinese human rights lawyers, whom PRC security personnel prevented from seeing the congressmen.[139]

In the 112th Congress, among other actions, Representative Chris Smith introduced the China Democracy Promotion Act of 2011 (H.R. 2121), "To deny the entry into the United States of certain members of the senior leadership of the Government of the People's Republic of China and individuals who have committed human rights abuses in the People's Republic of China, and for other purposes." Senator Robert Menendez introduced a resolution calling for an end to the persecution of Falun Gong practitioners in China (S.Res. 232). On May 13, 2011, the Subcommittee on Africa, Global Health, and Human Rights of the House Committee on Foreign Affairs held a hearing entitled "China's Latest Crackdown on Dissent." Representative Kevin Brady has publicly called for the release of U.S. citizen Xue Feng, a constituent from Houston, who remains imprisoned in China.

United Nations Human Rights Council

The PRC remains highly sensitive to foreign criticism, but has often been able to employ its soft power—diplomatic and economic influence—in international fora in order to reduce international pressure to improve its human rights policies. The United Nations Human Rights Council was formed in 2006 to replace the U.N. Commission on Human Rights (UNCHR), which had been faulted for being unduly influenced by non-democratic countries. The United States had sponsored several resolutions at the UNCHR criticizing China's human rights record, but none were successful; China was able to thwart voting on most resolutions through "no-action motions."[140] The Bush Administration had opposed the formation of the Council and declined to become a member, arguing that it did not offer improvements over the UNCHR and that it placed too much focus on Israel.[141] The Obama Administration sought and was granted a seat on the Human Rights Council in June 2009.

---

[138] Melinda Lu, "Saying No to Bush," *Newsweek*, November 22, 2005.

[139] Jim Yardley, "China Blocks U.S. Legislators' Meeting," *New York Times*, July 2, 2008.

[140] Since the U.S. government began sponsoring resolutions criticizing China's human rights record in 1991, they have been blocked by "no action" motions nearly every time. Only one, in 1995, was considered by the UNCHR, but lost by one vote. The last such U.S. resolution was introduced in 2004.

[141] See CRS Report RL33608, *The United Nations Human Rights Council: Issues for Congress*, by Luisa Blanchfield.

The United Nations established the Universal Periodic Review (UPR) mechanism by which the Human Rights Council would assess the human rights records of all U.N. members once every four years. The UPR Working Group conducted a periodic review of China in February 2009. Representatives of some countries voiced serious concerns about China's human rights record, while representatives of some developing and non-democratic countries expressed support of China.[142] The United States participated as an observer, but not yet a member, of the Council during China's review.

Human Rights Dialogue

The U.S.-China human rights dialogue was established in 1990. It is one of eight government-to-government dialogues between China and other countries on human rights. Beijing formally suspended the process in 2004 after the Bush Administration sponsored an unsuccessful U.N. resolution criticizing China's human rights record. The talks were resumed in May 2008, the first round in six years.

The Obama Administration has participated in two rounds, the fourteenth round held in May 2010 in Washington and the fifteenth round in May 2011 in Beijing. Both were co-chaired by U.S. Assistant Secretary of State for Democracy, Human Rights, and Labor Michael Posner and PRC Ministry of Foreign Affairs, Department of International Organizations Director General Chen Xu. In the 2010 meetings, topics included Chinese political prisoners, freedom of religion and expression, labor rights, the rule of law, and conditions in Tibet and Xinjiang. The Chinese delegation also visited the U.S. Supreme Court and were briefed on ways in which human rights issues are handled in the United States.[143] During the 2011 talks, Assistant Secretary Posner raised the Obama Administration's deep concerns about the PRC crackdown on rights defenders and government critics. Discussions of China's "backsliding" on human rights reportedly dominated the talks, which the U.S. side described as "tough" and Chinese officials portrayed as "frank and thorough." Posner characterized the dialogue process, however, as a forum for candid discussion, not negotiation.[144]

Although no breakthroughs or concrete outcomes were reported during the latest rounds, Administration officials have continued to perceive the dialogue as an important means by which to emphasize and reiterate U.S. positions on human rights issues. They have suggested that, given the deep disagreements on human rights and other contentious issues, the holding of the dialogue and the agreement to continue them represent positive steps. Furthermore, some observers have contended, the absence of the dialogue would undermine other U.S. efforts to promote human rights in China.

Some analysts have expressed concern that separating the human rights dialogue from the comprehensive Security and Economic Dialogue (S&ED) has marginalized human rights issues.

---

[142] Human Rights in China (HRIC), "China's UN Human Rights Review: New Process, Old Politics, Weak Implementation Prospects," February 9, 2009.

[143] Foster Klug, "No Breakthroughs in U.S., China Human Rights Talks," *Associated Press*, May 14, 2010; State Department Special Briefing with Michael Posner, Assistant Secretary for Democracy, Human Rights and Labor, May 14, 2010.

[144] Chris Buckley, "U.S. Ends Rights Talks With China 'Deeply Concerned'," *Reuters*, April 28, 2011; Assistant Secretary of State for Democracy, Human Rights and Labor Michael Posner, U.S. Embassy Press Availability, Beijing, China, April 28, 2011.

Some human rights experts have argued that the talks, which the PRC government has referred to as serving to "enhance mutual understanding," enable Beijing to deflect international criticism on human rights. They have suggested that the dialogue should be more transparent and made conditional upon measurable human rights improvements in China.[145]

Rule of Law and Civil Society Programs

During the past decade, the U.S. Department of State and the U.S. Agency for International Development (USAID) have administered a growing number and range of programs in China using foreign assistance funds. Between 2001 and 2010, the United States government authorized or made available nearly $275 million for such programs, of which $229 million was devoted to human rights, democracy, rule of law, and related activities, Tibetan communities, and the environment. U.S. program areas include the following: promoting the rule of law, civil society, and democratic norms and institutions; training legal professionals; building the capacity of judicial institutions; reforming the criminal justice system; supporting sustainable livelihoods and cultural preservation in Tibetan communities; protecting the environment; and improving the prevention, care, and treatment of HIV/AIDS in China. The direct recipients of State Department and USAID grants have been predominantly U.S.-based non-governmental organizations and universities.[148]

> ### Congressional-Executive Commission on China
>
> Between 1989 and 1999, the U.S. Congress sought to monitor and hold the PRC government accountable for human rights violations through the annual renewal of "most favored nation" (MFN) trading status. The measure that granted permanent normal trade relations (PNTR) treatment to China (P.L. 106-286), ended this mechanism, but included provisions on human rights. The PNTR act established the Congressional-Executive Commission on China (CECC) to monitor human rights and the rule of law in China and to submit an annual report with recommendations to the President and Congress.[146] Title III of the act provides that the Commission shall consist of nine Senators, nine Members of the House of Representatives, five senior Administration officials appointed by the President, and a staff of ten. The Commission provides human rights-related news and analysis, keeps track of pertinent PRC laws and regulations, and maintains a database of political prisoners.[147] Since its inception, the CECC has held over 80 public hearings and roundtables on rights-related topics. It has an annual operating budget of approximately $2 million.

National Endowment for Democracy

Established by the U.S. government in 1983 to promote freedom around the world, the National Endowment for Democracy (NED) is a private, non-profit organization that receives an annual appropriation from Congress. NED has played a major role in promoting democracy in China since the mid-1980s. Activities of NED and its core institutes include supporting Chinese pro-democracy organizations in the United States and Hong Kong, helping to advance the rule of law in China, promoting the rights of workers and women, and assisting the development of Tibetan communities. The Endowment's China programs have received support through the annual foreign operations appropriation for NED (an estimated $118 million in FY2010) and

---

[145] Information Office of the State Council, op. cit..; Li Xiaorong. "What I Told Obama About Beijing's Human Rights Problem." *The New York Review of Books*, January 18, 2011.

[146] P.L. 106-286, Title III, Section 301.

[147] See http://www.cecc.gov.

[148] For further information, see CRS Report RS22663, *U.S. Assistance Programs in China*, by Thomas Lum.

congressional earmarks to NED for democracy-related programs in the PRC and in Tibet. In addition, the Department of State has provided direct grants to NED's core institutes.[149]

Labor Rights

The U.S. government has encouraged PRC adherence to international labor standards. U.S. officials monitor PRC compliance with the 1992 U.S.-China Memorandum of Understanding and 1994 Statement of Cooperation on safeguarding against the export of products made by prison labor.[150] In 2000, the law granting permanent normal trade relations (PNTR) status to China authorized the Department of Labor to establish programs to promote rule of law training and technical assistance related to the protection of worker rights.[151] Since 2002, the Department of Labor has supported the following activities in China: rule of law development, labor rights, legal aid, labor dispute resolution, mine safety, occupational safety and health, and HIV/AIDS education. In addition, the governments of the United States and China, including the U.S. Departments of State and Labor, the PRC Ministry of Human Resources and Social Security, and the All China Federation of Trade Unions, have conducted exchanges and discussions on wage and hour (payroll) administration, unemployment insurance, pension security, labor market statistics, law enforcement, collective bargaining, and other issues.

Internet Freedom

The U.S. government has undertaken efforts to promote Internet freedom, particularly in China and Iran. In 2006, the Bush Administration established the Global Internet Freedom Task Force (GIFT). Continued under the Obama Administration, GIFT's duties are to monitor Internet freedom around the world; respond to challenges to Internet freedom; and expand global access to the Internet. [152] Congress appropriated $50 million for global Internet freedom efforts between 2008-2010 and $20 million in 2011. Program areas include censorship circumvention technology, Internet and mobile communications security, media training and advocacy, and public policy. The principal or target countries of such efforts are China and Iran. The Broadcasting Board of Governors supports counter-censorship technologies that help enable Internet users in China, Iran, and other countries to access Voice of America and other censored U.S. governmental and non-governmental websites. In March 2010, representatives Chris Smith and David Wu launched the Global Internet Freedom Caucus to promote online freedom of information and expression, followed by the founding of the Senate Global Internet Freedom Caucus, chaired by Senators Ted Kaufman and Sam Brownback. On April 6, 2011, the Global Online Freedom Act of 2011 (H.R. 1389) was introduced, "To prevent United States businesses from cooperating with repressive governments in transforming the Internet into a tool of censorship and surveillance, to fulfill the

---

[149] NED's core institutes or grantees are the International Republican Institute (IRI); the American Center for International Labor Solidarity (ACILS); the Center for International Private Enterprise (CIPE); and the National Democratic Institute for International Affairs (NDI).

[150] According to the Department of State, the U.S. officials monitoring China's compliance with the bilateral agreements on prison labor "receive very limited cooperation" from the PRC government. Bureau of Democracy, Human Rights, and Labor, *Advancing Freedom and Democracy Reports*, May 2010 (China).

[151] P.L. 106-286, Section 511.

[152] U.S. Mission to the United Nations in Geneva, "Press Release: Secretary of State Establishes New Global Internet Freedom Task Force," February 14, 2006. See also CRS Report R41837, *Promoting Global Internet Freedom: Policy and Technology*, by Patricia Moloney Figliola.

responsibility of the United States Government to promote freedom of expression on the Internet, to restore public confidence in the integrity of United States businesses, and for other purposes."

Public Diplomacy

U.S. public diplomacy programs expose Chinese educated elites and youth to U.S. politics, society, culture, and academia; sponsor exchanges; and promote mutual understanding. According to the Department of State, approximately one-third of all Chinese citizens participating in U.S.-sponsored professional exchange programs work in field related to democracy, rights, and religion. In 2009, 541 U.S. citizens and 948 PRC citizens participated in U.S. educational and cultural and exchange programs.[153]

International Broadcasting

The Voice of America (VOA) and Radio Free Asia (RFA) provide external sources of independent or alternative news and opinion to Chinese audiences. The two media services play small but unique roles in providing tastes of U.S.-style broadcasting, journalism, and public debate in China. VOA, which offers mainly U.S. and international news, and RFA, which aims to serve as a source for domestic news that Chinese media are prevented by censorship from covering, often have reported on critical world and local events to Chinese audiences. The PRC government regularly jams and blocks VOA and RFA Mandarin, Cantonese, Tibetan, and Uighur language broadcasts and Internet sites, while VOA English services receive less interference. Both VOA and RFA are making efforts to upgrade their Internet services and circumvention or counter-censorship technologies.

Surveys commissioned by the Broadcasting Board of Governors (BBG) have confirmed that its reach in China is relatively narrow but significant. Based upon 2009 data, the BBG estimates that roughly 0.1% of China's population listens to or views VOA radio, television, and Internet programs, or about 1.3 million people weekly. VOA "Special English" international news programs, aimed at intermediate learners of English, are popular with many young, educated, and professional Chinese. RFA's more targeted, politically oriented audience is estimated to be one-third to one-half of VOA's. Among foreign broadcasters, Phoenix (Hong Kong) satellite television enjoys the greatest public awareness (46%), followed by VOA (12%).[154] RFA is viewed in many dissident and ethnic minority communities in China as a vital source and outlet for news.

---

[153] U.S. Department of State, Bureau of Democracy, Human Rights, and Labor, *Advancing Freedom and Democracy Reports*, op. cit.; Interagency Working Group on U.S. Government-Sponsored International Exchanges and Training, *FY 2009 U.S. Government-Sponsored International Exchanges & Training Regional Report—East Asia and Pacific*. These totals include the following State Department programs: Post-Generated Exchange and Training; Citizen Exchange; Fulbright; Global Educational; International Visitor Leadership; Special Academic Exchange; Special Professional and Cultural Exchange; and U.S. Speaker/Specialist.

[154] Discussions with BBG staff; Office of Inspector General, *Report of Inspection: Voice of America's Chinese Branch*, Report No. ISP-IB-10-53, July 2010; Broadcasting Board of Governors, *Fiscal Year 2012 Budget Request*; "U.S. Plans to Lower Its 'Voice' in China," *Wall Street Journal Online*, February 17, 2011; "Congressional Battle Brewing over VOA Mandarin Service Cuts," *chinaview.wordpress.com*, February 17, 2011.

Author Contact Information

Thomas Lum
Specialist in Asian Affairs
tlum@crs.loc.gov, 7-7616

www.ingramcontent.com/pod-product-compliance
Lightning Source LLC
Chambersburg PA
CBHW081405170526
45166CB00010B/3217